ALWAYS DISCERNING

Other Books by Joseph A. Tetlow, SJ

Making Choices in Christ: The Foundations of Ignatian Spirituality

Choosing Christ in the World: Directing the Spiritual Exercises of St. Ignatius Loyola According to Annotations Eighteen and Nineteen

ALWAYS DISCERNING

An Ignatian Spirituality for the New Millennium

Joseph A. Tetlow, SJ

LoyolaPress.
A Jesuit Ministry

3441 N. Ashland Avenue
Chicago, Illinois 60657
(800) 621-1008
www.loyolapress.com

Imprimi potest: Very Reverend Ronald A. Mercier, SJ, Provincial

ISBN-13: 978-0-8294-4456-8
ISBN-10: 0-8294-4456-4
Library of Congress Control Number: 2016946119

Printed in the United States of America.
16 17 18 19 20 21 22 Versa 10 9 8 7 6 5 4 3 2 1

Contents

Acknowledgments and Dedication

A great number of people have contributed to these pages. Naming all of them would take too long, but here are the places they gathered: Jesuit Hall of St. Louis University, men who were real brothers to me at various periods over thirty years. The Institute of Jesuit Sources, particularly Frs. John Padberg and Claude Pavur. There, too, the Garfield Group of Frs. Chris Pinné, Albert Rotola, and Jack Hunthausen, who put up with much while the book was getting launched. BRIDGES, the program of *Exercises* in Daily Life in St. Louis, particularly Joan Felling and Mary Mondello. The "Cheerful Charlies," Jesuits who make our annual eight-day retreat in various wildernesses, especially John Stacer, Thomas Rochford, and Gary Menard. The Ignatian Prayer Pilgrimage Groups, held together in Dallas by Berta Montes and including Paul and Sally Pederson and Mike and Liz Bassett. The Ignatian Spirituality Institute of Dallas, Texas, created by Carol Ackels. And finally, Kavanaugh's Theologians in St. Louis, who let me listen to their discussions, masterminded by Joseph Lipic, Sr., my Friday Breakfast Companion.

I should add that every time I tell about an experience, or recount a story, I could tell about another or others like it. Some individuals are named in the narrative. Elizabeth Moulin is a therapist and spiritual director with whom I taught spirituality to ecumenical groups at Perkins School of Theology at Southern Methodist University. Eileen Rafaniello Barbella is also a therapist and spiritual director; we have worked together for thirty years. Joyceann Hagan goes unmentioned but gave us all a lot of help. So also Mary Allen Jolley, the best cousin in the world.

I am particularly grateful to the editors of Loyola Press, particularly Joseph Durepos, Vinita Wright, and Susan Taylor.

The book is done to honor the Lady Mary, Undoer of Knots, who has undone plenty as my life and this book unfolded, and to keep alive the memory of Donald L. Gelpi, SJ, philosopher and theologian, my incomparable friend.

What Is Discernment Now, and Why Do We Need It?

Discernment has become a constant in the lives of mature Christians. A lawyer in Connecticut says he often has to discern the morality of a legal action. The mother of grown children, who prays daily with Scripture, found herself living all day with a sense of God's Spirit with her; she told me that she was discerning what that meant. A young woman in Dallas asked me to pray with her as she discerned whether to go to a Catholic college. A couple in Seattle have been discerning whether to sell their home. As I write this at Grand Coteau, nine younger men, Jesuit novices, are discerning through the thirty-day Spiritual Exercises whether their vocation to the Jesuits is authentic. A lot of people I know discern steadily what God hopes in them.

Discernment is a gift offered to everyone who believes in Jesus Christ. Those growing into a spiritual life hear St. Paul: *Do not be conformed to this world, but be transformed by the renewing of your minds, so that you may discern what is the will of God—what is good and acceptable and perfect* (Rom. 12:2).

Pope Francis has certainly heard this. He is showing the world how a discerning mind and heart light up everything a follower of Jesus Christ does. He acts constantly in discerning ways, trusting instincts that have been honed over years by prayer and struggle (including failure). He not only does it, he talks about it. His conversations, as they are reported by those close to him, begin with listening. He has listened to the People of God—the little people, the educated people, the leaders civil and religious—and he has heard us reaching for discernment and finding this renewed spirituality for the twenty-first century.

In his exhortation *The Joy of the Gospel*, the pope talked about discernment twenty times. In a candid interview with a Jesuit editor, much briefer than the Exhortation, he used the word fifteen times—and explained what he meant by it. He summarized his thought on it this way: "Discernment is essential."[1] We can trust his actions and his teaching, which will show up a lot in the following pages.

Mature Christians, however, were growing more aware of this life-shaping charism well before Pope Francis was elected Bishop of Rome. We were applying it to moral choices, life decisions, and even the simple judgments of everyday matters. It is given us by *the Spirit of truth*, whom the unbelieving world around us simply does not know. But Jesus said to his followers: *You know him, because he abides with you, and he will be in you* (John 14:17).

We are still working to clarify all the things meant by *discernment*, however. During most of the past century, we thought of it principally as a way to discover God's will, particularly about being a religious or a priest. We tended to think that the people facing those decisions were the ones who needed to do this discernment thing. And for decades at the end of the past century, those who did it focused strongly on a specialized *discernment of spirits*—which was the only entry on it in the original *Catholic Encyclopedia*. Anyhow, it was mainly experts who were interested in it.

Then the Church—now seen as the People of God—was guided by the Second Vatican Council (1962 to 1965) to "read the signs of the times." That has led to broadening considerably what we mean by discernment. It has also led to expecting all mature followers of Jesus Christ to get into it. Fifty years after the Council, not only scholars and nuns and priests, but also all mature disciples are discerning. And we are giving the term clear and rather subtle meaning, as the many voices in these pages will show.

The pages will also show that I am aware of this historical development, but I am not recounting that history. I am interested here in what mature disciples mean when we say that we are *discerning*. The layers of that meaning begin in our being aware and appreciating that God is not our Creator a long time ago but is continually creating us, moment by moment. We have to explore this "first great discernment," in which we learn to appreciate our busy, intimate Maker. The next layer grows as we learn more about Scripture and early Church teaching. We learn that Jesus Christ is the Redeemer not only of the Church but also of all humankind. When we probe this "second great discernment," we need prayer to help us open our mature hearts to him as *my* Redeemer.

In this intimate dialogue with God, we have grown aware of the Holy Spirit, and we have begun appreciating that the Spirit is shaping us. This appreciative awareness opens us to consider how to discern the Spirit's work. Particularly through consolation and desolation, the Holy Spirit teaches this truth: "From a youth, I have molded you according to my liking." Not *your* liking—*my* liking.

Discernment in the real world of everyday life is not a computer game. The mature follower of Jesus Christ recognizes that sin has a role in this—my own sin, sin in us, and sin abroad in the world. We must look into what sin's consequences have wreaked: suffering, violence, and death. That will bring us to ponder how The Way is not the only one people follow, and how we must shake our way free from the other ways—of the world, the flesh, and the devil. The final brief notes explore what has clearly become an asceticism appropriate to our time.

As I began studying this charism during the last decades of the past century, we were going through the last throes of modernity. We have reached what Pope Francis says is not an age of change but a change of age. We still need the virtues of gentleness and self-mastery. But more than ever before, we need some other gifts of the Holy Spirit: wisdom, knowledge, counsel, and understanding.

If prayer has grown more shallow than it could be, here are some depths to plumb. If making the Examen has grown a bit vapid, here are keen things to look into. And anyone who wonders how the mature disciple of Christ can sensibly live joyfully in a world of spite and hate, division and violence, will do well to turn to discernment as the People of God are now practicing it.

Joseph A. Tetlow, SJ
Feast of Christ the King, 2015

Touchstones

- Discernment, once considered a specialist's concern, now goes on in every mature disciple's life.
- Pope Francis considers discernment necessary in every believer's life and shows how we are to do it.
- We discern when we come to experience God as our Creator and Lord at every moment of life.
- All of us who mature in discernment come to appreciate Jesus Christ as "my Redeemer."
- We discern the consequences of sin in our suffering and having to go through death.
- We live in joy as the Holy Spirit gives us the gifts of wisdom, understanding, and gentle self-control, and these give us a discerning heart.

PART ONE

FOUNDATIONS

1

"Appreciative Awareness" of God Acting in the World

It's fundamental that one thinks what one feels and does; feels what one thinks and does; and does what one thinks and feels. You must use the language of the head, the heart, and the hands.

—Arbp. Jorge Mario Bergoglio

People mean a lot of things when they talk about discernment. But the word names a distinctive experience—rich, clear, and deep in varying degrees. Discernment is more or less consciously employed when we are trying to reach meaning, or judgment, or decision and action. People who do not approach their lives with much conscious, spiritual intent will tend to discern only when something important comes up. Those who are more spiritually practiced will recognize that the experience we call discernment shapes ordinary incidents in daily life.

A mother in Cleveland listens to her teenage daughter as she tells what a joy it is to help an elderly neighbor go to Mass, Sunday after Sunday. The mother feels hesitant—there are considerations of prudence—but she senses grace at work in her daughter's joy and rejects fear. She has discerned what the situation is saying to her: the good thing to do is to rejoice in her daughter's generosity.

A young father in Baton Rouge is offered a challenging promotion in his company. As he sees it, the new position will require less travel and more time at his desk. Noting that he will be in a position of leadership, he remembers that Pope Francis called business a "noble vocation."[2] He also feels that the new job will deepen his joy in his work and give him greater freedom with his spouse and children. His wife agrees, and he accepts the new job.

One more situation: A couple in Dallas who have been asked to volunteer as instructors in RCIA have grappled in the past with struggles in faith and hope. But they distinctly remember being encouraged when others shared difficulties with doctrine or the new liturgy. Then they read a homily the new pope gave right after his election. About all the faithful, he said, "Those who listen to us and observe us must be able to see in our actions what they hear from our lips, and so give glory to God!"[3] This couple feels convinced that sharing their own experiences of faith and doubt will come as a grace to the adults who want to be baptized. So they volunteer—and as a result end up happily teaching others in the faith for years to come.

The first thing to notice in these examples is that the judgments and actions of these men and women come from faith-filled minds. They are good people, and even if they have not paid much attention to the theology behind their lives, they are living in the grace of Christ. They know in their heads that God cares for us always and that our Creator and Redeemer intends only our good. They belong to what Pope Francis calls "the saints of every day," whose lives are so ordinary that they are hidden in "a sort of 'middle class of holiness.' The middle-class saints know Jesus' rule of thumb: *In everything, do to others as you would have them do to you* (Matt. 7:12)."[4]

But their awareness is not merely in their heads. Rather, such awareness stirs hearts that believe the faith, appreciate it, and embrace its truth as their own. These men and women are living out an appreciative awareness of God acting in their lives. They know and are truly happy that *in him we live and move and have our being* (Acts 17:28). This is the mature Christian's mindset and what I have come to call their *heartset*. As one computer-age gospel commentator put it, it is their "personal operating system."[5]

> These men and women are living out an appreciative awareness of God acting in their lives.

Here's something else to consider: The experiences of that mother and young father, and the experiences of the couple, go beyond thinking and feeling. They are doing the truth lovingly (see 1 John 3:18). This is the third thing common to all these Christian experiences. Discernment names not a feeling merely, or something we have understood or determined through reason alone. These mature Christians have enacted their clear faith and their honest believing, in the hope that they were doing as Jesus did, *only what he sees the Father doing* (John 5:19).

To the extent that these individuals reflected on what they were doing and how they were doing it, they were discerning. Simply put, the experience that we call discernment is living with an appreciative awareness of the constant interplay of complex human realities we refer to as head and heart and hands. Our heads hold our faith—our memory, knowledge, and understanding of the truths of revelation. Our hearts hold our believing—our convictions, commitments, and yearnings in the love of God, whom we trust with our whole selves. Our hands express what we do, summarizing what we are making of ourselves and expressing and enacting through our character.

Each of these—head, heart, hands—affects the others and is affected by them. While he was still cardinal archbishop of Buenos Aires, Pope Francis told writers who were interviewing him, "It's fundamental that one thinks what one feels and does; feels what one thinks and does; and does what one thinks and feels. You must use the language of the head, the heart, and the hands."[6] This puts it succinctly and gives us a lot to think about.

• • •

Any discernment will be framed by our being aware of and interpreting "the signs of the times." We attend mainly not to what is going on among the nations but what is happening in our own "lifeworld," in this place and at this hour and in my own life. Discerning people keep aware of what is going on around them. We actually intend to view things the way Jesus did: God the Almighty is intimate in the tiniest creature and yet cannot be contained by the whole of creation. To understand this, Pope Francis said, is "to assume a correct position for discernment, in order to hear the things of God from God's 'point of view.'"[7]

As people who have placed our trust in God and in God's ongoing revelation to us, we choose not to take the world's point of view about what is pleasurable, profitable, or powerful. We grow aware of the Holy Spirit at work in our world. The more mature among us can see God at work in everything.

And the sum of all our desires is to live the love that God has poured into humankind—by loving those whom God gives us and by taking care of anyone whose need calls on our gifts.

This says quite a lot. We might wonder at this point why anyone would want to figure all this out. What calls us to this challenge?

2

The Author's Story of Discernment

The Jesuit always thinks, again and again, looking at the horizon toward which he must go, with Christ at the center.[8]

—Pope Francis

Most readers will know that it is natural for a Jesuit to be interested in discernment. We are trained from our first weeks as Jesuits to discern—like the novices across the campus now making their thirty-day retreat. And our training ensures that we keep this lifelong mindset and practice it day by day in our interior lives and in our work for the Church. Discernment drives the Jesuit "way of proceeding," as Pope Francis has demonstrated very clearly.

My interest in discernment started in 1947, when I was sixteen. I was finishing prep school, immersed in New Orleans jazz and the military aura of the nation's new role as a world superpower. My Jesuit high school was the unique U.S. Marine Junior ROTC. Our alumnus senator in Washington was chair of the Armed Services Committee, which might have had something to do with it. I entertained myself with a schoolboy dream of being an admiral in the navy or maybe a captain in the marines. Instead, I joined the Jesuits. My notions of life in the military and the Jesuits were equally vague and fanciful.

From July 1, 1946, and for the next two years of novitiate training, however, my notions of Jesuit life got real. I was schooled in discernment and guided rigorously to a well-weighed and well-pondered decision: it really was young Joe Tetlow who had made this commitment and not Joe Tetlow, nephew of a Jesuit uncle, graduate of a Jesuit school, classmate entering with classmates. I committed my life to the company called the Society of Jesus. I have never looked back.

id look back in some odd ways, and fairly promptly. We
ıanent commitment once and for all, as did the Son of
ıat we must do it day by day. Worse than that, I expe-
, the disease driving you to be sinless in order to prove that you are loveable, by God or anybody else. Back then, we spent two years studying the humanities. We spent all day studying Latin and Greek and modern languages, learning Western history and art, reading Shakespeare and Flannery O'Connor, singing in choir, and listening to great secular and sacred music.

Then we went to another university to study philosophy. I left my companions of four years behind and went alone to a huge Jesuit community of more than a hundred men studying theology and another hundred, philosophy, along with their faculties and staffs. There, we heard lectures in Latin, read texts in Latin, answered professors' questions in Latin, and took exams in Latin.

I took the disease of perfectionitis with me. Its fevers need discernment, because perfectionitis is a waiting room with doors opening to grave temptation. One door opens into discouragement and depression as we keep on sinning. Another door opens into vanity and pride when we start deciding for ourselves what is or is not a sin. And yet another opens into the emptiness of disbelief.

That last is the door I opened. While studying philosophy, I went through a period when I wondered whether I really believed in God—or rather, when I feared that I no longer believed in God. The experience was very dark and littered with sharp particulars. I remember the room I was standing in when my stomach sank and my voice said inside me, *What if there is no God? There is no God.* And on the table near my hand was a pair of white gym shorts. It was morning. I didn't talk to anyone that day.

I didn't talk much at all for a long while. I knew one hard particular: I had to stay where I was, a Jesuit. So my heart remained fixed even while my faith floated free. The experience was absurd, of course—it was full of contradiction and inanity. It might well have ended with another little agnostic running around declaring his freedom from religion. This all went on for some weeks or months. I told no one about it. But my father had chosen to believe in Jesus Christ and the Church, and my mother was a prayerful Irish Catholic. And one of the men in my cohort, Tom Shea, asked me in the gentlest voice, "What's the matter, Joe?" I can still hear him, sixty years later. I couldn't answer.

Then it ended. Simple as that. Obviously my experience of unbelief did not end with me in the intellectual prison of skepticism or atheism. What it ended with, by God's grace, was a realistic appreciation of the powers of the human mind. I was actually doubting not the existence of God but the power of the human mind to do what my faculty were teaching me it could do. They clearly implied that if I worked hard and thought clearly, I could reach unshakeable certainty that, in spite of all appearances throughout history, God lives and governs in might. I could prove God's existence absolutely, not once, but in five ways, and maybe six. And then I could live absolutely certain of doing God's will.

No. I did not and do not believe that. It is not what has been handed on to us. What has been handed on to us, deeply threaded through our own experiences of life and love, is God revealing himself. We live "in the unfathomable mystery of those who seek God and allow themselves to be sought by God," as Pope Francis put it in a homily.[9]

What has been handed on to us is *hope*. For as Francis added in that homily, "God reveals himself in the historical mystery of our movement through grace and sin." We live in the confident hope that Christ is Lord, that God is Love and cares about us and me. We trust that God knows our limits and sins better than we do, and forgives them. I have had to discern these realities over and over again, as everyone has. Each discernment ends in hope-filled enactment that doing the next good thing is what our Creator and Lord wants, and truly is, doing.

> We trust that God knows our limits and sins better than we do, and forgives them.

I mean to say in these pages that discernment is the way of living maturely in Christ in the new millennium, and all who have chosen to live in Christ will have to discern over and over again, just about every day, all our lives long. This is our asceticism, demanding prayer and practices that are likely to strike us as humble and penitential. It calls for passionate love and for humble detachment. Discernment will feel like the cross often enough.

My interest in discernment was forced on me by my life choice, my Jesuit life. But my interest turned to joy as spiritual friends have found themselves discerning, too. The Church—the People of God—has grown clearer and clearer during the past half-century that discernment is an act, and an attitude, and a necessary way of living maturely in Christ. So these pages will tell about many real people who live the discerning life. To guard confidentiality, of course, I change names and places and anything identifiable.

I have been involved in retreat giving, spiritual counsel, and spiritual direction since my ordination in 1960—and I have lived and worked as a priest in many places. Starting in Grand Coteau, Louisiana, I have lived and worked in Austin and Dallas, in Berkeley and Providence, in New York and New Orleans and Washington, D.C. Abroad, I've lived a long while in Rome and a shorter while in Murcia de la Nora in Spain. I have worked in seminars and retreats in Madrid, Manila, Taipei, Lima, and Dublin, and given spiritual direction in Harare, Zimbabwe; Chennai, India; and Kuala Lumpur, Malaysia. I write this in the Jesuit Retreat House in Grand Coteau.

One of my brothers claims I just can't keep a job. But I have kept walking with fellow pilgrims to God in Christ and have learned to love listening to them.

3

Discernment Is for Every Christian, Every Day

The wisdom of discernment redeems the necessary ambiguity of life.
—Pope Francis

At the beginning of the 1900s, the *Catholic Encyclopedia* defined *discernment* as the Ignatian "discernment of spirits." During that whole century, taking the *Spiritual Exercises of St. Ignatius Loyola* as the starting point, spiritual writers explored discernment as a formal process we go through to find God's will.[10]

At the time of the Second Vatican Council, we were all looking at discernment as a way of making big decisions. We could list the steps to be taken: fix a pure intention to find what God wants done; reject anything conscience objects to; consider the good alternatives, being careful not to be attached to any of them; weigh each of them in one of several ways; decide what to do; offer your decision to the Lord; enact it; then watch to see whether God approves by confirming you with consolation. This is how we were thinking about discernment. It had to do with decision making, particularly with big decision making.

We still discern serious decisions. But the Second Vatican Council has called on us to broaden our discernment by asserting that "the Church has always had the duty of scrutinizing the signs of the times and of interpreting them in the light of the Gospel."[11] We all rather quickly discovered what that "scrutinizing" and "interpreting" called for.

Cardinal Donald Wuerl, for instance, saw that ongoing conversion of heart "essentially involves discernment." He explained it this way: "Each of us Catholics must stop and see where the Lord is working and where there is room for growth."[12] He saw discernment in the working of our mature conscience. The English translation of the *Catechism of the Catholic Church* picked up this new insight and explained that we apply our consciences to everyday matters through "practical discernment."[13]

Beyond moral issues, if we are to interpret things in the light of the gospel, we have to go beyond textual criticism. As biblical scholar Luke Timothy Johnson sees it, we must turn to Scripture to "discern and respond with obedient faith to the work of the living God in the world."[14] Theologian Richard Gaillardetz reads Scripture "to penetrate ever more deeply the meaning of God's word" not only to grasp the truths of revelation but also to "discern the appropriate application of that word" to our everyday lives.[15]

This new approach to discernment encompasses not only the practical but also the larger vision of things. Dr. Eileen Rafaniello Barbella, a Catholic therapist with postdoctoral work in Ignatian spirituality, sees it as "a kind of spiritual vision, a capacity to see and comprehend the nature of reality." The mature disciple can "discern the truth of a situation" and not just what's to be done.[16]

Jesuit spiritual director Larry Gillick has listened to a lot of mature disciples of Jesus give evidence of having "a way of sensing what is going on all the time."[17] This implies that discernment covers not only thinking, feeling, and acting—but even just *being*. This is what Dr. Edmund Pellegrino claimed: Christians enjoy "the freedom to be and do what one discerns God wants one to be and do." Not just figure out *what to do*, but even *who to be*.[18]

• • •

These are surprising changes, and we have taken a while to grasp them. I have been listening for fifty years to people tell about their search for God. Like many others, I used to wonder what people meant when they said they were discerning. It was not Ignatian discernment of spirits—I was sure of that. I sometimes wondered whether it meant much at all. I gradually realized that I was not listening very well, for serious Christians have been using the term in sound and purposeful ways.

Most comprehensively, when we say that we are discerning, we mean that we have set ourselves to find God at work in the world and to unite ourselves to him. We are imitating Jesus of Nazareth in this. He said that *by himself, the Son can do nothing; he can do only what he sees the Father doing* (John 5:19, NJB). Isn't this what we mean by "doing God's will"?

When we say that we are discerning, we mean that we have set ourselves to find God at work in the world and to unite ourselves to him.

Put that way, it seems simple enough, and perhaps in everyday life it is simple enough. But it is not so easy to explain how "the wisdom of discernment redeems the necessary ambiguity of life," as Pope Francis put it.[19] It is a process, the ongoing interaction among our head and heart and hands. We are discerning whenever we are aware of the dynamic interrelationship among

- **head**—our grasp of the true faith revealed by Jesus Christ through the Church to us;
- **heart**—our belief in Jesus as our Savior and our commitment to living his Way; and
- **hands**—our behavior in ordinary life, the enactment of the faith and our belief in it.

These three—head, heart, hands—are always interacting, whether we are aware of it or not. As we mature in Christ, though, we grow more and more aware of how our ideas of the faith affect what we are committed to and what we do; how what we are committed to impacts our grasp of the faith and what we do; how what we do expresses and feeds back into our understanding of the faith and what we really want and value.

This is what we now mean by discernment, to which the entire Church is called as all of us read the signs of our own times and in our own places.

4

The Second Vatican Council and Signs of the Times

The Spirit pushes us to take a more evangelical path but we resist this. . . . Submit to the Holy Spirit, which comes from within us and makes us go forward along the path of holiness.

—Pope Francis

For the first time in the history of the Roman Catholic Church, an ecumenical council addressed not only the hierarchy and theologians but all Christians. The Second Vatican Council emphatically declared that "Church" means the whole People of God. To be sure that everyone understands, it addresses all of the faithful as *The Church in the Modern World.*

One of that document's urgent declarations came in the fourth paragraph: "To do its duty, the Church has constantly to read the signs of the times and interpret them in the light of the Gospel."[20] Our belief in Christ presses us to ask and answer for ourselves "the questions that humankind has always asked about the meaning of this life, about the life to come, and about our relations among ourselves." With that statement, the Council pushed the Church into living our faith with a discerning heart. This was, and is, an exciting movement in the Church as "the Spirit pushes us . . . along the path of holiness."[21]

As the Council ended in 1965, we all began enthusiastically "reading the signs of the times." The more liberal saw the signs of the times pointing one way and the more conservative, another way. In fact, the many different readings of the Council provoked dissatisfaction and even dismay. The truth is that no one had much of an idea fifty years ago what this "reading the signs of the times" really entailed, let alone how to go about doing it.

The expression "signs of the times" comes, of course, from Jesus of Nazareth. He brought his adversaries down to earth when they challenged him to show them "a sign from heaven." You look at a red sky, he told them, and know how to read what it says. In the morning, storms; in the evening, calm. *"You know how to interpret the appearance of the sky, but you cannot interpret the signs of the times"* (Matt. 16:3).

Popes began unpacking the phrase as soon as the Second Vatican Council ended. Pope Paul VI thought it had to do with teaching the faith. If we have evangelizing in mind, we will find "innumerable events and human situations" that give scope to "a discreet but incisive statement of what the Lord has to say in this or that particular circumstance."[22]

A bit more philosophical, Pope John Paul II looked at events for an invitation, "a 'call' which God causes to resound in the historical situation itself." He saw God acting: "In this situation, and also through it," God gives the believer a call, a summons to action.[23]

These pontiffs wrote about reading the signs of the times. In his exhortation *The Joy of the Gospel*, Pope Francis does read the signs of the times. His exhortation is one long exercise in reading and interpreting—*discerning*—the signs of the times. And every homily in *The Church of Mercy: A Vision for the Church,* the first collection of his homilies and talks, does the same: each reads the signs of the times from a Christian viewpoint.[24]

Further, Pope Francis goes beyond just understanding and interpreting. He points out that the Holy Spirit works in these signs to show us what to do—what next good thing awaits us. The pope does not see us getting this by theology or biblical studies or philosophy. In Pope Francis's mind, we are all to hear God's call and respond to it by *discernment*, a word he uses again and again.

By discernment, Pope Francis means the same thing that mature Christians mean by it. Discernment names the active search to find God working in me, in others, and in the world and to do what God is doing. Through discernment, we come to work with God working in the world: *We are well aware that God works with those who love him* (Rom. 8:28, NJB). And what is

God working at? The first pope answered that: God is shaping his people, *a chosen race, a royal priesthood, a holy nation, God's own people* (1 Pet. 2:9).

When we encounter this God, we encounter challenge. We have developed several maneuvers to avoid this challenge. We can keep God at arm's length by insisting that we make ourselves holy when we "observe certain rules or remain intransigently faithful to a particular Catholic style from the past."[25] This may drive the yen some have for attending the Mass celebrated in Latin by a priest with his back to the holy people. We can also keep God at the other arm's length by trusting ourselves to movements of self-realization and human fulfillment, to what Pope Francis calls "a spiritual consumerism tailored to one's own unhealthy individualism."[26]

When we encounter this God, we encounter challenge. We have developed several maneuvers to avoid this challenge.

Guided by the Spirit of Love, twenty-five hundred bishops at the Second Vatican Council confronted us with our call to holiness. All the baptized have "the dignity and freedom of the [children] of God, in whose hearts the Holy Spirit dwells as in His temple."[27] This might provoke Americans to irony (or despair), because in Western culture, we think we have to go find God. The facts are different, as Francis says, "because God is first; God is always first and makes the first move."[28] However many times we hear it, this comes as a surprise. Well, as Pope Francis went on to say, "God is always a surprise, so you never know where and how you will find him."

This is not a new insight. It is a foundational truth: *Love consists in this: it is not we who loved God, but God loved us and sent his Son to expiate our sins* (1 John 4:10, NJB). The first basic fact is that God seeks us and finds us. The next basic fact is that "you must, therefore, discern the encounter," as the pope put it.

And this is his last word: "Discernment is essential."[29]

5

Every Mature Disciple Discerns All Day Long

Over a long stretch of time we humans have been learning . . . how to recognize and respond to the face of God.

—Pope Francis

I tend to think that being a mature Catholic requires using our brains. Even the least educated among us acknowledges Three Persons in One God, which is pretty high theology. The humblest live believing that we are to share forever in the triumph of Christ Jesus. And in that light, every one of us weighs what might be the next good thing to do. Consequently, it's not that surprising that Christ's followers can grow to have a rather intricate understanding of discernment.

Though reflecting on discernment can become complex, practicing it is open to everyone who is willing to consider things prayerfully. The whole course of an experience of discernment might go this way:

- We come to an appreciative awareness of the concrete situation we are in: facts and values, opportunities and challenges. We see what is going on from the perspective of Christ's redemptive action.
- We evaluate what is going on in gospel terms, guided by the Holy Spirit, the Advocate whom Jesus sent from the Father *to be with you for ever* (John 14:16). In the concrete particulars of our situation, we find leads about what God is accomplishing.
- Then we decide what the next good thing might be for us to do. We do not find certainty. Rather, we find that God confirms our choice by consoling us, keeping us joyful even in ambiguous and tough situations. We "recognize and respond to the face of God."[30]

Think of a couple in their fifties who have three children, two already off on their own and one still at home finishing school. The couple have between them only one parent still alive: her mother. They see signs that finances and health issues add up to the mother living with them. They are aware of the drawbacks as well as the good points in such a move.

They then decide that the commandment to honor your father and your mother does not end at old age. Even though bothersome problems do arise about space, both physical and metaphorical, they ask her to come live with them, and she does.

Their decision leaves a lot uncertain, of course, but the uncertainties do not add up to doubting that they are doing God's will. As Pope Francis said, "in this quest to seek and find God in all things there is still an area of uncertainty."[31] We live and act in hope. And though we *may abound in hope by the power of the Holy Spirit* (Rom. 15:13) and our hope is a sure hope, nonetheless, when we make a judgment and reach a decision, our discernment continues. We continue aware of what we have done and evaluate our spirit's response to our decision. Pope Francis is quite emphatic: "Uncertainty is in every true discernment that is open to finding confirmation in spiritual consolation."[32]

This is what we expect of the mature disciple: that each brings a Christian appreciation to any situation. We perceive the "facts" from a viewpoint fixed in faith in an ongoing Creator of all things seen and unseen. We look at the available options hopefully and lovingly, expecting to find values for the present life that will go beyond merely avoiding sin. What we want is to grow continually in the *image* and likeness of a God who is love (Gen. 1:27). So when we come to decide what to do, we intend to *love, not in word or speech, but in truth and action* (1 John 3:18). This faith and belief give shape to every act we do discerningly.

Think about Mother Teresa (now St. Teresa). She goes to cleanse the sores of a leper, whom she sees as a person being created by God and being saved by the blood of Christ. This person's human dignity is reflected in Mother Teresa's radiant eyes, because she is washing the wounds, not of one more leprous body but of Christ's body. *Truly I tell you, just as you did it to one of the least of these who are members of my family, you did it to me* (Matt. 25:40).

Mother Teresa did not just sanitize a leper's lesions, though that certainly looked like what she was doing. She was actually taking care of Christ's Body as revealed in the leper she cleaned and loved. This was her discernment every time she took care of one of the poorest of the poor.

How many religious women have done that through the centuries, and in our own nation? And how many husbands and wives have cared for spouses with Alzheimer's or lingering cancers? When he ran an archdiocese, Bishop Bergoglio asked his priests to notice this: "In our Church, we have many saints with whom we deal on a daily basis: in our parish life, in the confessional, in spiritual direction."[33]

During any ordinary day, every follower of Christ makes many concrete choices. What we do looks like what everyone else is doing, even coworkers or neighbors who are agnostic or atheist. However, we bring to everything we do a faith that puts its deepest meaning into human experience of world and time. As Christ's followers who are aware, we do not simply act—we *enact*. We put into every action what our faith is telling us right now, what holy hopes we feel in this moment, and we mean to make every act an act of love for God and others and our own selves. The mature disciple of Christ looks like everyone else just the way a radioactive steel rod looks like any other steel rod. There's quite a difference.

As Christ's followers who are aware, we do not simply act—we *enact*.

Within our faith communities, we live the discerning life at various levels and intensities. We can keep from sin by obeying the commandments and living grateful for what God gives to us and does for us and around us. That requires the discernment of conscience. Or we can grow more mature and choose to try always to find what God wants in our time and place, discerning for ourselves not only *what is good and acceptable* but even what is *perfect*, what makes us more like Jesus of Nazareth (Rom. 12:2). Then we will be accepting what God offers to each of us: our encounter with God, himself, acting.

6

The Bare Bones of a Discerning Life

A faith that does not know how to grow roots into the lives of people stays barren. And instead of an oasis, it creates more deserts.
—Pope Francis

We can state now the bare bones of what mature disciples mean by discernment.

Every human person lives using head, heart, and hands. When we are baptized and begin to live in Christ, this doesn't change. But now faith "puts roots" into head, heart, and hands.[34] The dynamic gets charged by *Christlife* the way atomic energy charges power plants. In these plants, all the rules of physics apply to steel and concrete and electricity, but they are transmuted entirely by radioactivity. In somewhat the same way, discernment transmutes the very human working of our head, our heart, and our hands. We grow into it gradually, just as radioactivity goes gradually from less to more intense, from negligible to highly explosive.

Our current practice begins in the Second Vatican Council's great document *Gaudium et Spes, The Church in the Modern World.* There, the bishops called attention to the urgent duty of the Church to "read the signs of the times." By *the Church*, they did not mean the pope and bishops. They meant the People of God—all of us. We are all "the Church."

And by "signs of the times" they were not asking all of us to be historians and pundits. "Signs" are not just the events in the wide world or the long developments of human history. The bishops meant what we can see with our own eyes and feel with our own hearts. And "times" are not world events or Wall Street or Congress. The bishops meant the things that are happening to us in our everyday life on our own streets and in our city councils. The bishops were convinced that the Holy Spirit is at work in the world, all the time, and gives evidences of it.

As we live our religious lives in our own time and place, the experience we have of doing the next good thing and of working through what happens—that experience we are shaping by discernment, whether we are aware of it or not. The human person works with head and heart and hands. That work is charged, energized with grace, by our baptismal call. Now we can see what it is.

Discernment, then, engages our head, our heart, and our hands. So as mature Christians, we are in the act of discerning when we are conscious of the interplay among our knowing the truths of our **faith**, our **belief** that shapes the heart's convictions and commitments, and our **actions** that bring to life those convictions and commitments. Look at those one at a time.

The human person works with head and heart and hands. That work is charged, energized with grace, by our baptismal call.

The faith (head): We believe in God, Creator of heaven and earth, not once at the big bang, but continually. God makes me moment by moment. God is not The Force, or chance, or the godlings Wealth, Power, or Pleasure. God is our Father, aware of each of us and caring about us. For God is love, and Love has hopes for us (the commandments, our vocations) and has come among us in our own flesh. In Jesus of Nazareth, God lived humanly a life of love and service and then, after a bitter death, rose again in his and our flesh, and lives forever. God the Holy Spirit comes to us, forming us into a People who hold on to revelation and the Way and pass it down through the generations in word and worship and sacrament. Jesus Christ will come again, and we will live with him forever. This is our "mindset."

Faith is handed on to us. Belief is what we take into our hearts. Flannery O'Connor put it this way: faith is what you know is true, whether you believe it or not.

The belief (heart): We were baptized into Christlife, and we acknowledge the mystery of the Holy Trinity. We accept Jesus as our Savior, and we embrace the teaching of the Church. We believe and mean to follow Jesus' words, fulfilling them in loving prayer and service. We are appalled by some things condoned by our culture's media and mores, in sex and marriage, in friendship and finance. We are convinced that we can love one another, and we mean to try to love ourselves so that we can love others and, especially, God. We want earnestly to do what we must do, to help those who need help, and to live with peace of heart, as far as we are able. This is our heartset.

Belief is also handed on to us and formed in us. But we have to take it into our hearts and let it emerge in how we live our days and hours.

The actions (hands). We do good and avoid evil as much as we can. We keep the commandments as we understand them, and we try to do what the Church teaches. We wish we had a way of life that embodied all that we think and believe, so we keep trying. We live so as to die in God's good grace. We love those whom God gives us to love and be loved by. We know the joy of actually helping people in need with our own hands and hearts as well as our wallets. We act responsibly in our civil and business life and do what we can about shaping our lifeworld's politics (we vote). We wish well to every person on earth and dodge hating even the jihadists by praying for them and against their terrorism. We worship God in our hearts and in our parish church, regularly.

This is living a discerning life. As Jesus said: *If you know these things, you are blessed if you do them* (John 13:17).

Touchstones

- Mature disciples are aware that what we think, feel, and do are tightly linked in our mindset and our heartset.
- We discern about what is sin and what is not, as well as what is good, loving, and holy.
- Our ability to discern and our exercise of it grow and develop with prayer and practice.
- We stressed the discernment of spirits before the Second Vatican Council, but that changed with the mandate to "read the signs of the times."

- The Church expects every mature adult to read the signs of the times in our own lifeworld and to attend to the Spirit's leading in what happens.
- Pope Francis considers discernment essential to living a life in grace of "middle-class holiness."
- Discernment grows through our understanding of the faith, our commitment to Jesus Christ in the Church, and our doing the next good thing, lovingly.

A Leader and God's People

Cardinal Jorge Mario Bergoglio astonished everyone from the first moments of his election as Bishop of Rome. His way of proceeding was humble, down-to-earth, and always joined to Jesus Christ. His leadership has been reported on and analyzed incessantly since his first day as pope. Most secular writers are puzzled because, as the wisest and best-informed of them puts it, Pope Francis "seems driven by a passion to serve, not by a craving for status, money, or power."*

But we do well to notice more than Pope Francis's personal life and leadership style. We need to see past the glare of his popularity to wonder, *Who does Pope Francis think he is serving?*

In a sense, every page in this book will answer that question. But we can summarize it succinctly. Pope Francis sees the Church as a people on pilgrimage, walking together with Jesus in our midst. He sees us as a broken, wounded people, hurt by human excesses, governments' failures, violence, and selfishness. We are a sinful people, led by a sinful, repentant man. The Church is a field hospital, not a castle built on a hill.

But at our best, we are a joyful people, alive in a humanity redeemed from our sin. We are adopted daughters and sons of the Father, and we are God's Son's mission continuing in the twenty-first century. Unless we are arrogant and greedy, we live everyday saintliness. We are devoted parents, aspiring to remain faithful to the end. We are women quietly running hospitals and orphanages. We are drawn to receive Jesus Christ in the Eucharist. And we live with our eyes on eternal life and our hands on the next good thing to do.

The vast majority of us live what Pope Francis calls "middle-class holiness." We are one reason why Pope Francis, whose life is serving us, is so happy.

*Chris Lowney, *Pope Francis: Why He Leads the Way He Leads* (Chicago: Loyola Press, 2013), 7.

PART TWO

DISCERNMENT THEN AND NOW

7

Discernment in the Christian Way

We do well to keep in mind the early Christians and our many brothers and sisters throughout history who were filled with joy, unflagging courage, and zeal in proclaiming the Gospel.

—Pope Francis

Mature Christians stay mindful of the truth God has revealed to us. We commit our hearts to believing in Christ Jesus, and we live in communion with him in his Church.

What we are doing, the earliest Christians also had to do. They heard the truth proclaimed and listened to it. They believed in Jesus Christ and committed themselves to follow his saving Way. Then they had to enact their yes by changing not only beliefs and attitudes but also their way of living among and doing business with pagan neighbors. That led to serious struggles.

The struggles began over the interaction of law and grace. St. Paul wrote to the Galatians about twenty years after Jesus' resurrection. In these letters he begs these early Christians to ponder that God is working powerfully among them. He tells them to consider whether God *is doing this through your practice of the Law or because you believed the message you heard?* (Gal. 3:5, NJB). He implies that God accomplishes this through the message, of course. At the same time, the more thoughtful believers wondered what it meant that Jesus had not abrogated the law but fulfilled it (see Matt. 5:17). What did that mean?

The more conservative-minded insisted that Christians should keep the law and the customs that Jesus himself had lived by: every male to be circumcised, no eating pork, no marrying unbelievers, keeping the Holy Days, and praying in the Temple. The fulfillment came not by ignoring the law but by following it out of love for Christ—who kept it himself. That would transform practices that were basically earthy into spiritual ones, provided that they kept the practices faithfully.

The more liberal believers felt just as strongly that Jesus had fulfilled all the demands of the law, so that we needn't follow it any longer. He sent the Paraclete to us, so that *the Law's requirements might be fully satisfied in us as we direct our lives not by our natural inclinations but by the Spirit* (Rom. 8:4, NJB). So the Corinthians argued that they could eat meat offered to pagan gods, claiming that when it comes to food, they had the right to do anything. St. Paul had to point out that, well, yes, but *"not all things are beneficial"* (1 Cor. 10:23).

That helped a bit, but questions remained. When one spouse converts, must the couple separate because they are then *mismatched with unbelievers*? (2 Cor. 6:14) In civic life, is it wrong to do even a little business with someone who *is greedy*, or *dishonest, or worships false gods*? (1 Cor. 5:10, NJB) What happens when unbelieving friends come to supper: do they share the Bread and the Cup?

The struggle erupted into a public conflict in Antioch. When Peter first came to visit the new believers there, *he used to eat with the Gentiles* whatever was on their table. But then some very upright people from Jerusalem came, and Peter *drew back and kept himself separate for fear of the circumcision faction.* When Paul joined him and saw that even *other Jews joined him in this hypocrisy*, he *opposed Cephas to his face* (Gal. 2:11–13). The squaring off among bishops in the 2015 Synod on the Family seems to have good precedents in our history.

These early difficulties came with discerning how Christ's grace is given to us. How much does faith count, and how much does keeping the law count? St. Paul wrote to the Galatians the flat truth: *We have come to believe in Christ Jesus, so that we might be justified by faith in Christ, and not by doing the works of the law, because no one will be justified by the works of the law* (Gal. 2:16). That might have pushed back against the strict-observance

These early difficulties came with discerning how Christ's grace is given to us. How much does faith count, and how much does keeping the law count?

people in Antioch, but the problem was different in Rome. St. Paul had to write to them pointing out that just because we acknowledge Christ as our Savior does not mean that *we are free to sin, now that we are not under law but under grace* (Rom. 6:15, NJB). Well, wait a minute—if we're not under some kind of law, where's the sin? Discernment was not easy.

It still isn't. As we have come to see, the early Church began to see that we can rely on the judgment of people who lead notably spiritual lives. Just four years after his discussion with St. Peter, St. Paul wrote to the Corinthians: *Those who are unspiritual do not receive the gifts of God's Spirit*—chief among them, discernment—but *those who are spiritual discern all things* (1 Cor. 2:14–15).

• • •

So it has been from the earliest days: the dynamic among the faith proclaimed, belief in the heart, and their enactment demanded personal and communal discernment. This suggests that the subject of these pages is not a nice spiritual game, a bit of elegant lace on our baptismal gowns. Discernment is a serious obligation laid on every mature disciple by our faith and hope. We all need the prayer that St. Paul prayed for the Philippians: *that your love for one another may grow more and more with the knowledge and complete understanding that will help you to come to true discernment* (Phil. 1:9–10, NJB).

What we discern is this: when Christ fulfilled the law, he redeemed us by God's love. We are saved not *by* doing good works. We are saved *for* doing good works.

We Americans are a "do good" people. We give hundreds of hours to volunteering and millions of dollars to good causes. And we are humanly fulfilled by helping. So we disciples need to keep something clear: what our culture estimates humanly good and self-fulfilling may be quite wise. But that estimation is not what we mean by discernment.

We keep in mind that human wisdom is not what we live by. We keep this in mind because in our day, a lot of secular wisdom goes into our reflections on our identity and authentic self. Secular Americans have become a remarkably reflective people—surveyed and classified and catalogued. Commonly now, many people with little religion practice what they refer to as "spirituality." Further, the more thoughtful among us have renewed a commitment to keeping religion in society, which is provoking or is provoked by strident apologies for atheism.

This adds up to our needing discernment at least as much as the Corinthians needed it so that we can be as "filled with joy, unflagging courage and zeal in proclaiming the Gospel" as they were.[35]

8

Corinth's Church: Faith, Belief, Enactment

Let us learn also from the saints who have gone before us, who confronted the difficulties of their own day.[36]

—Pope Francis

Christian experience in St. Paul's Corinth was as complex as ours is here and now. Its population mixed Greeks, Phrygians, Phoenicians, and Romans—many of them military personnel and their families. The Jews had very active synagogues, and the elegant pagan temples were fronted—of course—with Corinthian columns. Corinth had always been crucial to trade, a center of it in their world as New York City is in our world. Its Isthmian Games were second in importance only to the Olympic Games in Athens.

When Paul first went there, he went *in weakness and in fear and in much trembling*, partly because it was one of the most important cities in Greece (1 Cor. 2:3). But partly also because he knew he would run into plenty of expert teachers and philosophers (as he would in today's America). He was concerned that they might cause problems for the many who are not *wise by human standards* (1 Cor. 1:26). So he stayed there longer than he stayed in any other city. He found out that the "wise" were indeed causing problems.

They kept it up after Paul left. The Christians had divided into factions, worse than our conservatives and liberals. One would say, "I follow Paul"; another, "I follow Apollos"; another, "I follow Cephas"; still another, "I follow Christ" (see 1 Cor. 1:12). St. Paul got exasperated with them. He dismissed their wisdom and declared their discernment fraudulent. They were mere debaters (see 1 Cor. 1:20). Ouch. The Corinthians lived wide open to ideas and brought their interests into the faith, just as we bring counseling techniques, management skills, political tensions, clericalism, and feminism into ours. They faced a confusion that is common enough now: "I don't know what to believe anymore" or "I don't know what the Church teaches anymore." This is what happens when we drift away from a discerning spirit.

Like all the other early Christians, Corinthians faced hard issues about food, marriage, and religious practice that could get them confused about the truth. When he first preached in Corinth, St. Paul knew he could not speak to *you as spiritual people, but rather as people of the flesh, as infants in Christ* (1 Cor. 3:1). But he would not let them stay immature; they *were called into the fellowship of his Son, Jesus Christ our Lord* (1 Cor. 1:9). The Church in the United States—I mean the People of God—is waking up to this same call.

No one will hear that call who does not appreciate who and what we are. St. Paul could ask us, too: *Do you not realize that you are a temple of God with the Spirit of God living in you?* (1 Cor. 3:16, NJB) When we do realize this, we have matured in fellowship with the Son of God. Pope Francis stresses this fellowship by urging "constructive dialogue in facing the present moment." He underlined this for Brazilian cultural, political, and religious leaders shortly after his election: "When leaders in various fields ask me for advice, my response is always the same: dialogue, dialogue, dialogue."[37] He is adroitly leading the bishops in the same way.

Like all the other early Christians, Corinthians faced hard issues about foods, marriage, and religious practice that could get them confused about the truth.

Accepting this faith into our hearts gives a Christian a *sensus fidei*, an instinct for the faith. The International Theological Commission calls it "the personal aptitude of the believer to make an accurate discernment in matters of faith." That makes each of us, with our unique *sensus fidei*, "a vital resource for the new evangelisation to which the Church is strongly committed in our time."[38]

The truth does not exist in the world apart from us who are called to be partners with the Son just as the Corinthians were. Jesus said that he is the truth, and we are to imitate him by becoming that truth—even we American consumers—chosen in *the mysterious wisdom of God* (1 Cor. 2:7, NJB).

Here is a basic reality about mature Christian life: each of us is accountable for the truths we know and how we believe them. The discerning person can feel confident of being orthodox. Jesus put the reason for that quite vividly: *The good person out of the good treasure of the heart produces good, and the evil person out of evil treasure produces evil; for it is out of the abundance of the heart that the mouth speaks* (Luke 6:45). This underscores what discernment has been and still is, because discernment is not only about what we think and what we believe, about head and heart. It is also about hands, about what good we do. What we do proclaims what we think and what we believe.

A long generation after Jesus' resurrection, St. James made this a main point in his letter, insisting that faith by itself, if it is not accompanied by action, *is dead* (James 2:17). Among us today, it's easy to go to Mass on Sunday and contribute to good Catholic works and then go to work on Monday not only in the same clothes as everyone else, but also in the same mindset. Mature disciples have to do better than that.

The challenge is not just in each of us. It also comes from what is going on in our lifeworld. St. Paul had to write the Corinthians as many as four times as new questions rose. New questions arise for us, too. It is true that the creed we recite during Sunday Mass summarizes our faith. It puts a solid, unchanging foundation under a discerning life, and the mature disciple is likely to recite it in the morning as the day starts.

At times, however, we need the faith unpacked a bit: How do Adam and Eve fit into evolution? How are we to think about those among us with homosexual desiring? Is it acceptable to use contraception? What about the ordination of women? May we think about deliberately ending a terminally ill life? The summons we now feel from the Holy Spirit to take discernment seriously means that we need to do some studying on our own. If mature businessmen and women keep up on developments, can a mature disciple of Jesus Christ do any less? For this reason, we always need good teachers of the faith.

Believing, however, calls for more than mere exposition. Belief calls for holding the truth in the heart as well as the mind, being convinced of it and committed to its promises. And when we hold the truth in our minds and commit ourselves to it, we *enact* it. Abraham not only heard but also "received the call to set out for a new land."[39] St. James says that Abraham's faith and his actions were working together, and that's how we know he believed (see James 2:22).

Each of us believes. The convictions we feel shape the truths we hold—and both are shaped by what we actually do about them. This interaction goes on constantly. When we consciously experience that interaction and govern it, we are living a discerning life.

Some of us are better at discernment than others. Gifts differ. But the Church now expects all mature Christians to "read the signs of the times" in our own situations, places, and times. That is, to discern.

9

Discernment in "Middle-Class Holiness"

With the cross it is impossible to negotiate, impossible to dialogue: the cross is either embraced or rejected.

—Pope Francis

It must be clear by now that reflective, prayerful men and women make the fullest, richest discernments. But every mature disciple must practice discernment to some extent just to remain faithful to Christ. We know that sound ideas shape behavior, and so do prejudices. We know that good habits affect our thoughts and feelings, and so do sinful, impulsive acts. In other words, even when we face temptations to sin, we have to attend to the flow of energies among head and heart and hands. This is how we *discern what is the will of God* (Rom. 12:2).

Finding the will of God might seem to have been easier in times past, when all across the nation, families integrated our faith. So did our neighborhood life. The faithful demonstrated vibrant faith and hope in regularly going to Mass and in the great works of creating Catholic schools and hospitals. As people practiced their religion freely and willingly, no one thought they were discerning anything, but their steady dedication radiated a kind of ordinary holiness. As Pope Francis pointed out, even before the Second Vatican Council, we thought it "a wonderful thing to be God's faithful people."[40]

During the decades before the Second Vatican Council, we thought that discernment was the business of nuns and monks and priests. But by the beginning of this millennium, we had come to see that doing the will of God demands discernment of every adult disciple. We might be careful to note that Catholics who don't seem to be doing it are actually practicing discernment in everyday affairs and all the time.

Begin, perhaps, with the formal teaching of the Second Vatican Council that every Christian has a supernatural sense of the faith which "is aroused and sustained by the Spirit of truth"[41] This *sensus fidei*, the holy people's grasp of our religion, reaches not only to believing the revelation made by Christ, "but penetrates it more deeply with right thinking, and applies it more fully in daily life." Ordinary discernment begins in the work of our consciences.

The *Catechism* explains it this way. Our consciences begin their work with the "perception of the principles of morality." We then apply these principles to what we are doing "by practical discernment of reasons and goods; and finally judgment about concrete acts."[42] The perception of moral principle has long been thought of as a kind of intellectual instinct to grasp innate universal moral principles, called *synderesis*.

Now, some of the faithful keep the commandments and do not seem called to develop an interior life any further than that moral discernment. Or if they have the call, they do not hear it. We can think of them as reversing a current fad: they have religion but no spirituality. All the same, ordinary Christians, living ordinary days, at least implicitly make the fateful choices God asks all make: *See, I have set before you today life and prosperity, death and adversity* (Deut. 30:15).

People who claim that they do no more than keep out of sin at least acknowledge this as a challenge and make the choice more or less intensely. But if they embrace faith and good deeds to any extent at all, they have discerned what God wants for them here and now. They may even have some of the joy Christ brought us, at least "as a flicker of light born of our personal certainty that, when everything is said and done, we are infinitely loved."[43] Perhaps abuse and a negative self-image prevent some from feeling that. Nonetheless, every person who sincerely believes in the Holy Trinity, the Holy Catholic Church, the communion of saints, and the forgiveness of sins, and lives with *the hope which is stored up for you in heaven*, has made a vague discernment that we are created for life and prosperity (Col. 1:5, NJB).

• • •

We are correct to feel that any people who worship regularly rank firmly among those whom God chose *from the beginning to be saved by the Spirit who makes us holy and by faith in the truth* (2 Thess. 2:13, NJB). Even when our young people drift away from practicing the faith and the wisest course is to pray for them and show them mature joy, we still have to be careful to keep this in mind: "Every human being is the object of God's infinite tenderness, and he himself is present in their lives."[44] This is true whether or not they know it—or like it.

By wanting simply "to do God's will," we cement our relationship with God in holy intimacy. Now, intimacy reaches differing levels and degrees in friendship and matrimony. Intimate spouses might live the closest intellectual companionship, always sharing ideas. But plenty of couples have very different educations and hardly ever talk serious ideas. They enact their communion elsewhere and otherwise. So it is with each of us and the Lord. The Spirit gives each what light, holy feelings, and desires he wills. Before time was, *each of us was given grace according to the measure of Christ's gift* (Eph. 4:7).

> By wanting simply "to do God's will," we cement our relationship with God in holy intimacy.

Almighty God chooses how each of us will live knowing the Three Persons. As long as we are not deliberately refusing God's love by deadly sins against his commandments—adultery, vengeful hatred, grand theft—we essentially are doing God's will. This necessarily entails encountering God acting, God doing, and God creating and saving at every moment and all the time—though some of us hardly ever, ever think about that. Do we see here the magnificence of just doing the next good thing? Every time we are simply *wise in what is good, and guileless in what is evil*, we are achieving God's reign over humankind (Rom. 16:19).

The Holy Spirit stays in every one of our hearts and incessantly teaches us to think with sober judgment, *each according to the measure of faith that God has assigned* (Rom. 12:3). We do not create our relations with God. No, we are utterly and in every way God's making. We can all reach deeper discernment, of course, as we work through disappointments and disorientations and let go of distorted ideas. And every disciple of Jesus Christ will face the cross, and then there is no compromise. "With the cross it is impossible to negotiate, impossible to dialogue: the cross is either embraced or rejected."[45]

Then, in failure, illness, and tragic happenings, every one of us will have the same task: cling to Jesus Christ. In some measure, current talk about spirituality is in fashion, and fashions come and go. But *Jesus Christ is the same yesterday, today, and for ever,* and the faithful disciple's way of living in Christ—whatever the Father has determined and shaped—will carry each of us into life *forever* (Heb. 13:8).

In a prophecy that the Word of God fulfilled, Deuteronomy declares that *the word is very near to you, it is in your mouth and in your heart for you to put into practice* (Deut. 30:14, NJB). There it is: head, heart, hands. St. Paul said it another way for the Romans: *For one believes with the heart and so is justified, and one confesses with the mouth and so is saved* (Rom.10:10). All who cling to Christ Jesus and remain in grace are precious in God's eyes. We can believe that they belong among the middle class in holiness. To believe otherwise is to yield to the dark.

10

Discernment in Jesus' Parable Telling

Let us not say, then, that things are harder today; they are simply different.
—Pope Francis

Jesus was traveling with his disciples—the Twelve, Magdalen, Joanna, Suzanna, and others—and found people misreading the signs of their times. Some of those who heard Jesus accepted him, like the scribe who asked about the greatest commandment. But many had their hearts set on their own ideas and practices, and these kept them from taking Jesus' words into their hearts and acting on them. Jesus could be blazingly clear when someone needed it, as he was with those Pharisees who were doing a lot of harm. But he also knew that ranting could turn away those who were struggling to grasp the meaning of his wonder-working. They even needed to know that he understood the struggle.

So he told them the parable about the sower who sowed seed along a path in a field where good soil was sprinkled with rock and shallow places. We have heard it explained a lot of times, but maybe we could look at it again. It can help us grasp how all of us are called to discernment all the time.

As often happened, the disciples weren't sure they got what Jesus was driving at. They waited until they were by themselves to ask him, as they often did. (What VP wants to ask the boss in public to explain a basic company policy?) Jesus told them directly: *To you it has been given to know the secrets of the kingdom of God; but to others I speak in parables, so that "looking they may not perceive, and listening they may not understand"* (Luke 8:10).

We could wonder now why this obvious lesson is one of the secrets of the kingdom of God. Perhaps it has to do with why a smart man like Christopher

Hitchens can hear the Good News and not get it. Jesus makes it plain: we are given the consolation of both hearing his voice and taking his teaching into our hearts. The discerning disciple stays aware that not everyone is so blessed, and that even when we struggle, we need to be grateful that our hearts are open to God.

The Sower, of course, is the Lord, and the seed is the truth being offered—the faith. Some people hear the truth the way a paved walkway takes seeds: seeds bounce and birds trounce. *The ones on the path are those who have heard; then the devil comes and takes away the word from their hearts, so that they may not believe and be saved* (Luke 8:12).

> Some people hear the truth the way a paved walkway takes seeds: seeds bounce and birds trounce.

The nonbelievers around us are plenty smart. But wealth, pleasure, ambition, and success harden hearts and close them. And even where these cultural forces have not yet reached, secular culture wraps us all in individualism that makes it very hard to share another's faith and hope. This opens the way to disbelief: going solo. It's the way plenty of Catholic college students follow as they are educated to think for themselves. As they leave their homes, they are tempted to leave their families, too—and the values their families embodied. They go solo and suffer what Pope Francis calls "a growing deterioration of ethics, a weakening of the sense of personal and collective sin."[46] These developments "have led to a general sense of disorientation, especially in the periods of adolescence and young adulthood, which are so vulnerable to change." It is a hard path.

Many American Christians live between the rock of secular culture and the hard place in which their developing lives are situated. They may think they hear the word loud and clear. They would like to love it. But when the time comes to enact what it demands, they cannot—or, at least, do not—persevere. It was hard in Jesus' lifetime, and we can't say "that things are harder today; they are simply different."[47]

A man married for about ten years attended a workshop on Christian manhood I gave at Cedarbrake Retreat Center in Texas. When he got home, his wife told me later, he talked for two hours. It was like before they were married. Then came Monday. He went back to a medical supply company and a job that demanded discerning ends and means. It also meant managing big egos and dubious material. So he came home at night taciturn, and that was the end of Christian manhood. *The ones on the rock are those who, when they hear the word, receive it with joy. But these have no root; they believe only for a while and in a time of testing fall away* (Luke 8:13). When these people are our family members, we have to remember that "Jesus offered his precious blood on the cross for that person."[48]

His story might just as well illustrate the next situation Jesus talked about. *As for what fell among the thorns, these are the ones who hear; but as they go on their way, they are choked by the cares and riches and pleasures of life, and their fruit does not mature* (Luke 8:14). Mature people today talk about Muslims or Chinese or Hispanics with a hardness that comes from a marble heart. They absorb the racism and nationalism infecting our culture the way iron absorbs radioactivity, and they do not love as Jesus loved. Work and worry, cuisine and television—these all distance us from God's peace. Living among these thorns, to use current sports talk, we live *dissed*—disgusted, distracted, disconnected.

Some of the thorns are in our Church policies. Many American Catholics spend most of their religious capital fighting government over abortion or birth control. At times, it seems that pastors focus so much on these that they become "obsessed with the disjointed transmission of a multitude of doctrines to be insistently imposed," which leaves good people a bit disoriented. What's the Good News about?[49]

But as for that in the good soil, these are the ones who, when they hear the word, hold it fast in an honest and good heart, and bear fruit with patient endurance (Luke 8:15). Here's the discerning life: understand the faith, embrace it honestly and well, and just keep doing the next good thing.

Touchstones

- The early Christians had to practice discernment, untangling law and grace, religious identity, and civil identity. We face the same tasks.
- Early Christians had plenty of conflicts, and even Peter and Paul contended.
- St. Paul wrote to the early Christians, hoping that their love would lead them to mature discernment.
- Every faithful disciple has a graced sense of what has been revealed and can trust a good heart.
- We who live in union with Christ are saved not
  by good works, but
  for good works.
- Some who believe in Jesus Christ seem to be called to live a simple religion following the commandments and enacting Christ's reign in our lifeworld.
- The Parable of the Sower can illustrate different levels of discernment and what makes enduring holiness.

Thinking about Experience and Discernment

One of the subtlest changes a pope from the Americas has brought to our Catholic spirit is the shift from laying stress on absolute unchanging truth to laying stress on tentative, changing experience. The former promotes explaining and defending the truths of revelation. The latter promotes a new Christian humanism, ideas and convictions that are "not abstract provisional sensations of the spirit, but represent the warm interior strength that renders us able to live and make decisions."*

Discernment in the twenty-first century is all about experience. All experience is in concrete context, and our fundamental context is the Mystical Body, the Church of the People of God. This pope, like the three before him, points out that the Holy Spirit is showing us in the "signs of the times" what God wants us to do.

Every experience begins with the perspective taken, and our perspective is a radical change from the nonbelievers'. We want to see things as God sees them—as this pope says over and over—from the perspective taken by Jesus of Nazareth.

Experience, next, is shaped by and shapes what we perceive and can perceive. Discernment asks that we perceive every person as God's work of art. It asks that we live aware of God's care for us in every instant. Next, our values shape what we can perceive and also what we can desire. Hence, we Christians value all things in the light of the Son of God's emptying himself to embrace our humanity. We can now realistically desire what he made possible: our destiny to live forever with God.

Finally, all experience is shaped by the decisions we make and the consequent habits of thought, feeling, and action. This is very plain in each one's experience: good habits give rise to good thoughts and feelings. This pope begs the discerning to recognize that humankind's decisions about our earth and sky have had widespread impact on our planet.

Mature discernment creates in us "the warm interior strength that renders us able to live and make decisions" like Jesus of Nazareth's and pleasing to the Father.

*Pope Francis, Address to the Fifth Convention of the Church in Italy, November 10, 2015.

PART THREE

GOD, ALWAYS OUR LOVING CREATOR

11

The First Great Discernment: God Is My Creator at Every Moment

But above all, I also know that the Lord remembers me. I can forget about him, but I know that he never, ever forgets me.

—Pope Francis, *Big Heart Open to God*

My niece Tania Christine had her first baby at forty, when she was already a professor in a highly ranked law school. She had experienced politics in Washington and had prosecuted cases in federal courts. When I went home to baptize the baby, Tania held her up and said that she had learned something new. She had never had the slightest notion of how utterly another person can depend on you, for everything, all day long and all night, too. My heart was about to sink, but then I saw, in her dawning, radiant smile, how she felt about this. She was delighted, absolutely delighted.

That mother was sharing an experience with God our Creator. For God, who is all Love, is radiantly delighted that we depend on him. All the time, *the LORD will again take delight in prospering you, just as he delighted in prospering your ancestors* (Deut. 30:9). As that mother delights that her baby depends on her, so does God delight that we depend on him—for everything, all day long, and nighttime, too. And the Lord "remembers me" and "I know that he never, ever forgets me," but smiles radiantly and steadily on each one of us.[50]

Our faith goes beyond the (correct) negative, "There is a God and it is not me." Our faith goes further to affirm positively that the almighty Creator of all things is always acting and creating; *he himself gives to all mortals life and breath and all things* (Acts 17:25). But God is not The Force: *God is love* (1 John 4:8). Our infinite, all-powerful God comes to us radiating the love of a parent—our Creator and Lord who is delighting in us. This is our faith.

Our infinite, all-powerful God comes to us radiating the love of a parent—our Creator and Lord who is delighting in us.

We know that we believe that faith when we have brushed aside all submission to or anger at fate, all agnostic trust in chance or luck, and all immature fear that God is an angry, vengeful force. This heartfelt, tender feeling that almighty God comes to us as our Father is the beginning of mature discernment. The Holy Spirit by whom *you have been anointed* tends to us the way that a young mother tends to her baby (1 John 2:20, NJB). And the Son makes us his brothers and sisters, *letting us be called God's children—which is what we are!* (1 John 3:1, NJB).

Be clear: we discern this only with reflection and prayer rooted in what the faith teaches. Some who do not have the Spirit's gifts of wisdom and understanding might figure that the mathematical proof that time began with the big bang and the scientific evidences of evolution seriously dent our belief that God creates. Why would it? Whether in that first single blowup or during the long unfolding eons, God is always creating, at every instant, all that exists.

Our faith gives us another truth about creation. *God created humankind in his image, in the image of God he created them; male and female he created them* (Gen. 1:27). God made the big bang, unfolding space and place and creating time. God called into being each creature, giving to each thing body and place and a measure of time. Through unimaginable eons, God kept shaping the cosmos and all its galaxies according to his eternal intention (which we perceive as his plan), until the elements of earth were ready to bring forth a life destined to be immortal.

Then into an animal of mud and earthly energy, destined to remain always earthly, God breathed a soul that is immortal. God was creating evolution all along, but this was a new thing. An animal—walking upright and with opposable thumbs and a large brain—was given what had never before existed on earth: a life that originated in but would not end in mud and earth, but instead would continue a living being into eternity.

The first men and women were glorious beings. *And the man and his wife were both naked, and were not ashamed* (Gen. 2:25). Why would they be ashamed? Each one's yearnings and desires were perfectly matched to the other's. Each one's pleasure was the other's as well. And both delighted in their own and their partner's splendor.

This is what the faith teaches about the human person: we are created in God's image. Consider: how can we be in God's image? Well, God is intelligent: thinking, imagining, planning; humans are intelligent: thinking, imagining, and planning. When we think and plan, we are thinking and planning along with God.

Next, God acts in freedom, choosing and refusing; we humans act in freedom, choosing and refusing. And when we act in freedom, we are acting with God, which lays the root to "finding God in all things." Further, God is creative, sharing divine life and making all things; we are creative, begetting children and making things. Whenever we create, including our own selves, we cocreate with God.

A final point about being in God's image: God is not the Force or fate. God is Person: Father, and Son, and Holy Spirit—always relating one to another and among themselves. In their image, then, we are related—generations, parents, siblings, spouses, loves—always related. None of us exists a mere solitary "I" except in illusion or in a mind game like Descartes's. No, each of us is intricately woven into "we."

And it is worth noting here that "male and female he created them" tells us that there is in God what is male and what is female, and we are in that likeness. So a father's seed cannot call forth life except with a mother's womb, and a mother's womb cannot call forth life except with a father's seed. And we now know that their offspring will always inherit from the two their physique and much else, concretized in a characteristic and unique DNA.

The first great discernment begins in our faith that God our Creator and Lord is calling us into being moment by moment and shaping us in the divine likeness as complete enfleshed spirits, as whole persons. And as God is love, we know that God delights in us as a mother delights in her child. This is an encompassing, personal relationship between our nothingness and the Creator of the earth and all the stars.

This is what our faith says. Now we discern how we go about believing all of it with our whole hearts and acting like we do.

12

Love of God and Love of Self

The Creator can say to each one of us: "Before I formed you in the womb, I knew you" (Jer. 1:5). We were conceived in the heart of God, and for this reason "each of us is the result of a thought of God. Each of us is willed, each of us is loved, each of us is necessary."

—Pope Francis

What changes in my heart when I really *believe* that God creates each of us moment by moment? I might understand in my head the teaching that God is incessantly Creator, but my heart might still be set on being "authentic" and in control of my own life. How does that change when I *have become obedient from the heart to the teaching*? (Rom. 6:17).

For most, it begins with self-acceptance: accepting myself as I am and living content with what my life has brought. St. Paul said that Jesus never hesitated: *in him it is always "Yes"* (2 Cor. 1:19). Jesus of Nazareth accepted himself as the Father was creating him: the Galilean child of Mary of Nazareth and Joseph, son of David. Jesus faced a life fulfilling *the promises . . . made to Abraham and to his offspring*—and the prophecies about the suffering servant (Gal. 3:16). And he was content.

I can know that I really *believe* that God is creating me as I am and loves me as I am, when I am saying a great yes to myself, content with my life. A constant flood of books urges upon Americans the idea of self-acceptance, from the *Self-Esteem Workbook* to *The Biblical View of Self-Esteem, Self-Love, and Self-Image*.[51] The idea is that I can be happy and flourishing as long as I accept who I really am.

These are helpful, but they do not describe a truly Christian heart. Our discernment brings home to us that I accept who and how I am not because it makes me happy and amiable—sometimes it does not—but because of my faith. "We were conceived in the heart of God, and for this reason 'each of us is the result of a thought of God. Each of us is willed, each of us is loved, each of us is necessary.'"[52] This "thought of God" is not yesterday or last year; it is now.

I can know that I really *believe* that God is creating me as I am and loves me as I am, when I am saying a great yes to myself, content with my life.

God in eternity is creating me in this moment and cherishing me as I am. And the Spirit moves us to yet another depth. For if God loves me the way I am, God loves me too much to leave me the way I am with all my flaws and sins. "God's saving love . . . is mysteriously at work in each person, above and beyond their faults and failings."[53]

Living in that belief frees us from the secular mindset of our culture. My happiness does not depend on what happens to me in health, wealth, and sex. My happiness depends on believing in God the way the servant of God Walter Ciszek believed in God. This American Jesuit missionary to Russia was arrested as a spy, tortured, and put to brutal labor in Siberia for twenty-three years. Risking his life, he kept hearing confessions and secretly celebrating Mass. He had been thought dead when he was suddenly released and returned to the United States in 1963.

He explained in *He Leadeth Me* how he survived all of this and came back free of rancor and resentment. He kept "a single vision, God, who was all in all; there was but one will that directed all things, God's will."[54] With this faith, he set his heart "to discern it in every circumstance in which I found myself, and let myself be ruled by it." He had learned from the gospel that God is everywhere sustaining all creatures in existence. "To discern this in every situation and circumstance, to see his will in all things, was to accept each circumstance and situation and let oneself be borne along in perfect confidence and trust. Nothing could separate me from him, because he was in all things."

This holy man was imitating his Lord, Jesus of Nazareth. For Jesus said plainly: *My Father is still working* (John 5:17). And he saw the Father's will in everything: *Very truly, I tell you, the Son can do nothing on his own, but only what he sees the Father doing; for whatever the Father does, the Son does likewise* (John 5:19). When we say that we want to "do God's will," what do we really mean? God's will is not just a label we put on what we do. We mean that God is working in what we do, before us and behind us, through us and around us.

Here we see the first of the several ways that believing the teachings of our faith affects what we do. We recognize that God is doing what we are doing, and what we are doing, God is doing. We are building the reign of Christ by doing the truth lovingly. A father patiently bails out his faltering twenty-year-old. A grandmother extends mothering to grandchildren in their two-job home. And all of us become "greens," because we know that we are now the "mind of the earth," the project of this planet and probably the fate of lots of other planets out there where we are sure to go.

Believing this brings us to the thrilling truth that God takes the initiative. We could never have made it up. It is almost unimaginable that we are actually doing the Creator's work. When we sing, we are creating beauty with God (well, some of us). When we cherish a spouse, we are bringing divine love into time. When we educate others, we are furthering God's project of a knowing, loving people.

As the mature come to the discernment that God is seeking us before we seek God, we have to open our hearts, alert and ready to realize when we are encountering God. For "God is always a surprise, so you never know where and how you will find him," the Pope says. We may think we are setting the time and inviting God into our space. No: God is waiting for us when we get there. "You must, therefore, discern the encounter."[55]

How do we learn to discern an encounter with God? By prayer—the kind of prayer that leads to a contemplative attitude.

13

God's Gravity and Galileo's Grapes

A contemplative attitude is necessary.[56]

—Pope Francis

Disciples living in the busy world have to grow into a contemplative attitude. We do this by praying the way Jesus told us to pray: *consider the lilies of the field* and *the birds of the air* (Matt. 6:28, 26). This prayer of consideration is about life's busyness and does not seek to leave or escape it. Instead, it grounds what Pope Francis calls "a contemplative gaze, a gaze of faith which sees God dwelling in their homes, in their streets and squares."[57] The Jesuit pope learned this prayer through the *Spiritual Exercises*, in which St. Ignatius instructs us to *contemplate* eighty times and *consider* sixty times—most commonly weaving the methods together.

Mature people can prayerfully consider any serious matter, like choosing the school for their children or electing to have a mammogram or PSI test. Done quietly in God's presence, we frame this prayerful consideration in our faith and hope in Christ and from it determine the next good thing to do. Then we offer our decision and our action to the Lord. In our busy culture, we never come to the end of things to think through and judge and talk with the Lord about. By this prayer—best thought of as the prayer of consideration—"God's gift becomes flesh in the culture of those who receive it."[58]

Jesus' friends surely took up this prayer. St. Paul, for instance, urged the Romans to consider what our present sufferings are compared to our future glory (Rom. 8:18). He instructed the Corinthians to consider that God chose not the powerful but the humble to do his work in the world (1 Cor. 1:26). The letter to Hebrews asks Jesus' followers to *consider that he was faithful* the way Moses was—and continues to compare things one to another (Heb. 3:2).

We have to look to natural forces and events to find evidences of God's ongoing creating. This might seem at first like making something up, a kind of mind game. But it is not, for God's presence cannot be "contrived" but must be "found, uncovered." It may be invisible to the naked eye, but "God does not hide himself from those who seek him with a sincere heart."[59]

Here is a good example: compare the force of gravity to the steadiness of God creating. All day long, at every minute, the earth is pulling me down, holding me to itself. The earth never lets me go, not for an instant. It is pulling everything else down too, especially my cell phone when I drop it. But gravity's hold on me is not indifferent to me. It is entirely personal: it is holding *me*. God called the cosmos out of nothing with a big bang, and out of that chaos, God is calling *me*, equally. (Well, no big bang.)

There is equality in gravity, too, as Galileo intuited. Drop two objects of different sizes and weights, he argued. Were there no atmosphere, they would land simultaneously. Centuries later, he was proven right by the astronauts. The moon has no atmosphere, so David Scott dropped a hammer and a feather at the same time. Sure enough, they landed just about together, for gravity pulls each thing equally, no matter its substance or shape. You can take that to illustrate how God works in each of us equally, keeping us equally alive and thinking and doing—no matter our sex, IQ, weight, or the condition of our soul.

Earth pulls me down, and God pulls me up, to put it that way—constantly, tirelessly, and personally. Should the earth ever somehow stop holding me down, I would fly off into space and *poof!* no me. It is this same way with God: if God ever stopped caring for me, I would simply not be. But we don't worry: nothing and no one will ever *nullify the faithfulness of God* (Rom. 3:3).

How often do we think about gravity? I asked this question in a lecture, and a voice promptly answered "this afternoon—teaching geography class." But even when we are not in geography class, gravity holds us to the earth.

And God holds us up too. Whether we are aware of it or not, God is loving us to life.

Galileo said something about grapes and the sun that gives us another comparison for God's constant caring. The sun, he said, holds all the massive planets in their orbits. Yet it pours its full energy onto a bunch of grapes as though that were the only thing it had to do. It is that way with God: still creating all the galaxies of the cosmos, God's infinite attention focuses entirely on each of us as though we were his only concern.

As Jesus knew, the sun gives us another comparison. When I stand out in it, I take its full light and heat. It gives me its whole energy and holds nothing back of all its rays and power. It will blind me if I let it and can burn me to a crisp. Well, like the sun, God comes to me in infinite energy and warmth. But there's a difference. The sun must shine with all its might on everything; that's all it can do. But God, with "a tenderness which never disappoints," measures his approach exquisitely to each of us, even the most sinful.[60]

While creating all the galaxies of the cosmos, God's infinite attention focuses entirely on each of us as though we were his only concern.

God's care, though, is as total as the sun's shining. Pope Francis insists, "God is in every person's life" just the way the sun shines on everyone. "Even if the life of a person has been a disaster, even if it is destroyed by vices, drugs or anything else—God is in this person's life."[61]

Furthermore, what is true of the sun—it was Jesus who pointed this out—is also true of the rain. For our Father in heaven *makes his sun rise on the evil and on the good, and sends rain on the righteous and on the unrighteous* (Matt. 5:45). When it rains, we all get equally wet, the only limit being how big or small we are. God's love is that way. His love is infinite and falls on all alike. The only limit is how big and open our hearts are.

In the last days it will be, God declares, that I will pour out my Spirit upon all flesh (Acts 2:17). For the discerning with a contemplative attitude, this is a most joyful prospect.

14

Discerning the God of Love

No one can strip us of the dignity bestowed upon us by this boundless and unfailing love.

—Pope Francis

St. Paul told the Athenian intellectuals about God in Christ that *in him we live and move and have our being* (Acts 17:28). Paul was quoting a Greek poet who had lived centuries before Christ and who had intuited only a profound, unsearchable mystery of a creating god. What the Greek could not discover through reason has been revealed to us: we live in love. We live in and for—and shaped by—a love vaster than all the cosmos and all times past and future.

This love is not a force. It is Three Persons—Father, Son, and Spirit—who live in perfect union yet remain each a distinct Person. Our faith is clear: "The very mystery of the Trinity reminds us that we have been created in the image of that divine communion."[62] Sin separated us from it; Jesus redeems us from sin and brings us again into that profoundly mysterious union. *As you, Father, are in me and I am in you, may they also be in us* (John 17:21).

When we really accept this gift of faith, we believe more than that God is present to us. We believe that God is *working* in us and through us, in our lifeworld. Jesus believed this so keenly that he could say honestly: *I tell you, the Son can do nothing on his own, but only what he sees the Father doing; for whatever the Father does, the Son does likewise*, a saying we have to go back to again and again (John 5:19). Mature discernment brings us this same conviction: unless we are sinning, we are doing God's will. We are coworkers in the Holy Spirit, and we are creating the kingdom the Father dreams of. And "no one can strip us of the dignity bestowed upon us by this boundless and unfailing love."[63]

Appreciating that we are coworkers, we learn who we are and who God is as well. This is the common experience in prayer: deepening in self-knowledge and deepening in divine knowledge go together—and only together do they grow deeper. We all grieve over our limitations more than we rejoice in our gifts until we accept that we do not make ourselves entirely on our own. God is doing it in and with each of us. Quite late in life, as I went into a chapel at dawn, I heard this in my heart: *From a boy, I have molded you to my liking.* Emphatically not to *my* liking but to *God's* liking—even mysteriously with my sins. God likes me with my sins! Not "in spite of" them; not "except for" them—just this: God likes me with my sins!

This is the heart of the first great discernment. The religiously mature reach it, but only with prayer. Some disciples do not reach it completely, just as some do not reach intellectual maturity with study and reflection or sexual maturity with generous love and good boundaries. Some do not reach moral maturity, either, but are content to do what everyone else is doing. This is deadly in a secular culture full of men and women whom St. Paul called *unspiritual* and who consequently *do not receive the gifts of God's Spirit.* At best, their discernment stays with earthy conscience matters, so they do not live mindful of God's urgent presence and actions, which *are discerned spiritually* (1 Cor. 2:14).

We all grieve over our limitations more than we rejoice in our gifts until we accept that we do not make ourselves entirely on our own.

• • •

We differ in how maturely our discernment reaches into God's intimate relationship. Very probably, we differ even in our giftedness to reach it. God our Creator and Lord really does call each of us as individual persons. But the mature discerner knows that God is active in the life of every person of any lifestyle whatsoever, even the most degraded and abandoned, endowing each one of them with the dignity of God's personal, unfailing love.

Surely, however, God leads every believer in Jesus Christ to the conviction that "God loves me as I am." This gracious gift is a special blessing for Americans who suffer insecurities and negative self-image. We are given the grace in our teens if we are well-reared in our faith. Some come to it only as adults. And those who have been abused (a multitude among us) can suffer deep feelings of worthlessness. They find it hard to live content that God loves them as they are. I listened recently to a mature priest grieve how he had been abused as a boy: "Where was God when this went on?" He had a fierce struggle to open his wounded heart and let the Spirit teach him that the Father is with his sons even when they are being abused—even when they are being crucified.

That priest had to reach what Jesuit priest Walter Ciszek called the "single vision"—the understanding and appreciation—that God directs all things. Fr. Ciszek had to discern in solitary confinement and forced labor what the faith said to him about being a prisoner for Christ—and what was the next good thing to do. "I looked no longer to self to guide me, relied on it no longer in any way." Instead, he renounced trying to have "control of my life and future destiny" and lived remarkably calm.[64] Through long prayer in solitary confinement and a lot of bitter suffering, he accepted the grace that nothing would shake his hope and love, not *the world or life or death or the present or the future*, because he heard in his heart that *all belongs to you, and you belong to Christ, and Christ belongs to God* (1 Cor. 3:22).

This discernment of God's all-pervasive creative love is a powerful religious experience. It is not likely to be the first discernment anyone makes. It was not mine. I had discerned quite a number of things before growing aware that God is making me moment by moment—always and in everything my Creator. I had discerned, for instance, that my gifts led to commitment not in matrimony but in celibacy. I had only a few ideas (almost all mistaken) about what that would make me. I did not know how the Holy Spirit would shape me as a priest any more than a man or woman knows how the Spirit will shape him or her as a spouse. We come to learn what God is making us as we commit ourselves to a real love and keep enacting it for better and for worse.

Most of us live this discernment securely only after being tested by disillusionment or discouragement. As Jesus of Nazareth did, we come to know who we are to be through the cross.

15

Loving God Is Who We Are

Accepting the first proclamation, which invites us to receive God's love and to love him in return with the very love which is his gift, brings forth in our lives and actions a primary and fundamental response: to desire, seek and protect the good of others.

—Pope Francis

When we make the first great discernment, we appreciate that God momently creates all things, like the sun shining on the earth and gravity holding all and each of us. As our discernment deepens, we can also come to appreciate something about returning God's love. We love God "with the very love which is his gift."[65]

Now consider that response. Our faith starts with the revelation that *God is love* and that we are in his image and likeness—which is the same as saying that we are created to love. Love is who we are. We are authentically ourselves only when we are loving, and we really know God only when we are loving. *Whoever does not love does not know God, for God is love* (1 John 4:8).

Believing this and then enacting this gift of love involves risk, both in our interior life and in our relationships. When we turn everything over to God, we do not know where God will lead us and who we will grow to be. Think of Teresa of Ávila, a busy little woman who became a great reforming saint. Think of Ignatius Loyola, beginning middle age by walking (limping) away from everything he had cherished. Think of the Lady Mary and her Son, Jesus of Nazareth. They all let love grow them into what they became.

When we regular people find life getting difficult, we can be tempted by an evil spirit to feel that the call to total love is a heavy burden. When our gifts demand labor and selflessness, we can balk. But feeling God's love as a burden is like an electric bulb complaining that electricity "makes me hot!"

Electricity enables it to give light to others the way God's gift of love enables us to give our love to others. God's gift is love for me; God's gift of love to me is for others.

My regretting my gift of love because it shapes me to be for others—mind and heart and hands—would be like Ella Fitzgerald regretting her voice because she had to sing songs. It's like Gerard Manley Hopkins grousing that to write his deeply spiritual poetry, he had to use spikey, weird English words. My gifts of mind and heart give me the voice and the words to love. To feel God's love as a burden is to complain about who we *are*.

But feeling God's love as a burden is like an electric bulb complaining that electricity "makes me hot!"

This raises the second risk we take when we truly accept God's gift of a loving heart—it "brings forth in our lives and actions a primary and fundamental response: to desire, seek and protect the good of others."[66] This response goes far beyond merely doing good for people we know, and it goes beyond fighting for social justice.

Such love goes beyond doing and helping to being: "God's word teaches that our brothers and sisters are the prolongation of the incarnation for each of us."[67] Here is the truth that Jesus declared when he said that whatever we do to even *the least of these who are members of my family, you did it to me* (Matt. 25:40). I cannot doubt that this insight is a mystical experience even if we don't float off the ground when we realize it. This theological truth is tough and quotidian. Jesus made that very plain: how we measure goodness to others is how it will be measured to us. If we are merciful to others, we will receive mercy. If we judge others, we will be judged. If we forgive, we will be forgiven. These sayings are so familiar to us that they have lost their force.

The mature will keep praying such sayings, however, because "going forth from ourselves towards our brothers and sisters" proves to be "the clearest sign for discerning the way to spiritual growth in response to God's completely free gift."[68] Holiness, the response to God's free gift, is not best illustrated as an hour of adoration in front of the Blessed Sacrament. That may not even illustrate it well.

For the Scriptures are not just about our individual relationship with God. They do not tell us to live for "an accumulation of small personal gestures to individuals in need, a kind of 'charity à la carte.'"[69] The Scriptures are about the kingdom of God, about God's plan for "gathering up all things in Christ, things in heaven and things on earth."[70]

We have to live in hope of a coming kingdom, but we also have to live aware of the kingdom already come. "God wants his children to be happy in this world too"—all of his children. In the Father's love all and through the Incarnate Son, "each human person has been taken up into the very heart of God."[71] Hence, our faith cannot be locked up into each private life, because accepting it in our hearts "always involves a deep desire to change the world, to transmit values, to leave this earth somehow better [than] we found it."[72] This is not romantic idealism or socialism. It is faith doing justice. It is Christian hope.

The first great discernment done maturely does not just obey but also fulfills the great commandment, *You shall love the Lord your God with all your heart, and with all your soul, and with all your strength, and with all your mind*, and the second that is like it, *and your neighbor as yourself*, each and all of us together continuing the incarnation of God in human flesh (Luke 10:27).

The Scriptures show us that this is not a pipe dream by giving us the model of it: Jesus of Nazareth. He is enfleshed divine love, love walking and talking and eating and sleeping. He is the splendid fulfillment of God's project in human nature: a human utterly integrated into his lifeworld and society, keenly self-aware yet utterly absorbed in and by the divinity. He is who we are meant to become. St. Paul experienced the mystery this way: *it is no longer I who live, but it is Christ who lives in me* (Gal. 2:20).

That truth moves us on to the second great discernment.

Touchstones

- God takes delight in his creatures—particularly in those who can take delight in him in their turn.
- God our Lord is incessantly our Creator—always creating us, at each moment of time.
- God creates us to share in the divine intelligence and freedom, creativity and love.
- Our first response to God's ongoing creation is saying yes to who and how we are, trusting his persevering care for us.
- We can see that we are "doing God's will" because God is working in and through us.
- We do not begin this: God is first; God is always first.
- We consider our faith that God is always acting, just as gravity is always acting.
- God's ongoing creating has the reach of the sunlight and the rain.
- In our maturity, we know that the love we feel for God, for others, and for ourselves is, itself, the gift of God's boundless and unfailing love.

Loving Like God

This is how love is in God. The Father gives himself utterly and entirely to the Son. He loves the Son in himself and finds delight in what is common to them: being God. The Son accepts being God from the Father and exults in it. Yet the Son loves the Father for himself. In what they share, each finds in the other a reflection of himself. They love the Spirit in being God, and in her turn, the Spirit accepts their love and delights and exults in the communion of love. God is love. This total self-giving, done once and forever, is a divine prerogative.

But then the Son emptied himself, not clinging to godhead but becoming like us. We have to recognize that divine love—in the image and likeness of which is our love—poured itself out. Pope Francis said that we will see "nothing of his fullness if we do not accept that God emptied himself."*

We cannot give ourselves once and for all. We must give ourselves to another in love again and again and again. And we all know keenly that we fail sometimes. We fail God, and God's love suffers for that. We fail one another, and our love suffers for that.

Even in the face of this, we live joyful lives, loving and faltering, in the confident hope that we will be saved by the love of Jesus Christ our Lord.

*Pope Francis, Address to the Fifth Convention of the Church in Italy, November 10, 2015.

PART FOUR
JESUS IS (MY) LORD

16

The Second Great Discernment: Jesus Is Lord

In union with Jesus, we seek what he seeks and we love what he loves.
—Pope Francis

Jesus told the disciples, *I am the way, and the truth, and the life* (John 14:6). They did not understand that very well. James and John, for instance, wanted Jesus to use his power over nature to zap with lightning the Samaritans who refused them a drink of water. Jesus must have just stared at them: a lightning bolt was not his way of sharing truth and light. The disciples had heard Jesus say that he is the way, the truth, and the life. But they had to learn how this worked out day to day.

All of us have to learn. Our faith teaches us that Jesus Christ is the universal Savior. I can believe that without letting him make much difference to me. This is where the second great discernment begins: I learn to believe that Jesus Christ is Savior *for me*. My Savior is not a remote and cold theological truth but the only one who can save me from my sin and carry me through my death to life. Meanwhile, he is the only one who can show me how to live as my Creator wants me to live.

He said that himself. *Learn from me*, he told his disciples (Matt. 11:29). We learn to "seek what he seeks" and "love what he loves."[73] We learn to embrace "Jesus' whole life, his way of dealing with the poor, his actions, his integrity, his simple daily acts of generosity, and finally his complete self-giving." We want to do that because all of this "is precious and reveals the mystery of his divine life."[74] As

My Savior is not a remote and cold theological truth but the only one who can save me from my sin and carry me through my death to life.

St. Augustine pointed out, the Son of God came to share our human nature so that we could share his divine nature.

Our Christian faith teaches us that Jesus Christ is both God and man. *He is the image of the invisible God, the firstborn of all creation* (Col. 1:15). Hence, the man Jesus of Nazareth shows us how the almighty Maker of heaven and earth thinks, feels, and acts, *for in him all the fullness of God was pleased to dwell* (Col. 1:19). Here we discern the root of all Christian belief and morality; everything grows from this great grace by which we are being formed in the likeness of incarnate love, Jesus of Nazareth.

This is the second discernment not because we are likely to make it at the very beginning of our religious lives, directly after accepting God's ongoing creation. No: it is second because my whole life in grace really unfolds when I, myself, embrace Jesus Christ. But I come to make this discernment as I mature humanly and mature in knowing and imitating him. Every one of us must let him "break through the dull categories with which we would enclose him" and humbly accept how "he constantly amazes us by his divine creativity."[75]

St. Paul saw that as we mature in discernment, we are brought to put on *the mind of Christ* realistically and in everyday life (1 Cor. 2:16). For the Word comes to us not merely as truth but as power and as the Holy Spirit and as full conviction (see 1 Thess. 1:5). Through the grace of our faith, we have a power of knowing that does not show up even in some good, highly intelligent, and esteemed people. It is humbling to realize that, as Paul said, *the god of this world has blinded the minds of the unbelievers* and they are unable to accept *Christ, who is the image of God* (2 Cor. 4:4). In our case, the light of faith we have accepted lets us believe that Jesus of Nazareth is the image of God and that he is the way we will learn how to be in the likeness of God as we have been told we are.

And as we accept in our minds and take into our own hearts what Jesus teaches, we begin to think and feel as he did. *Let the same mind be in you that was in Christ Jesus* (Phil. 2:5). This is how discernment works—but there is more. If we really do intend to think as he thought and to feel as he felt, we will meet the necessary condition—to live as he lived. This means that we try to act as Jesus did, all our actions firmly rooted in love.

We are facing here what holy people in the Church have long called "the imitation of Christ." But we did not think this up on our own; imitating Jesus Christ is not an idea some great repentant sinner invented. Jesus put it plainly. *While the disciple is not superior to teacher, [the] fully trained disciple will be like [his] teacher* (Luke 6:40, NJB). He was talking about himself, and he was talking about us.

The more mature our discernment, the more clearly we recognize that love is the key to imitating Jesus of Nazareth. *Just as I have loved you, you also should love one another* (John 13:34). This goes dead against the individualism and alienation of secular culture. When we love as Jesus did, "our lives become wonderfully complicated and we experience intensely what it is to be a people, to be part of a people."[76] We do not retreat into our comfortable cocoons. Instead, Pope Francis says, "Moved by his example, we want to enter fully into the fabric of society, sharing the lives of all, listening to their concerns, helping them materially and spiritually in their needs, rejoicing with those who rejoice, weeping with those who weep; arm in arm with others, we are committed to building a new world."[77]

When this second great discernment is made by those who lead a cloistered contemplative life, it may lead to a mystical union with God. When ordinary, busy people make this second great discernment, it regularly leads to a life full of good works such as helping in food kitchens, rearing children tenderly, and doing business in strict honesty. We are introducing a new humanism, a "Christian humanism which is born from the humanity of the Son of God."[78] His people do this "not from a sense of obligation, not as a burdensome duty, but as the result of a personal decision" to be like Jesus of Nazareth.[79]

This demands a strong self-appreciation and an equally strong selflessness in behavior. It will not happen apart from a life punctuated by the prayer of consideration and petition. So St. Paul wrote his friends in Philippi, *This is my prayer, that your love may overflow more and more with knowledge and full insight to help you to determine what is best* (Phil. 1:9–10).

17

Discernment Prepares Us to Encounter Jesus Christ

Being a Christian is not the result of an ethical choice or a lofty idea, but the encounter with an event, a person.
—Pope Benedict XVI

Among all the things revealed to us, "what shines forth is the beauty of the saving love of God made manifest in Jesus Christ who died and rose from the dead."[80] It is possible to believe revelation in Christ and then do little more than attend Sunday Mass and receive communion. This is the way of the religiously immature. Mature Christians go beyond that to realize that Jesus showed us "how to live well," because he lived "a life that had profound meaning, that imparted enthusiasm, joy, and hope."[81]

How do we develop this openness to encounter Jesus of Nazareth? The first step is to accept the fact that he has chosen to encounter each of us. *You did not choose me but I chose you* (John 15:16). In the reaches of eternity, God the Father has given us to Jesus Christ as his sisters and brothers. This is a sublime dignity that cannot be taken from us by any evil force, though it can be marred by selfish sin. God the Father's decision, Jesus said, is *that I should lose nothing of all that he has given me, but raise it up on the last day* (John 6:39).

As we grow in our discernment, we find three ways to open ourselves to this "encounter with an event, a person."[82] The first is the word of God. We find Jesus of Nazareth in the Gospels. The same Holy Spirit who shaped Jesus' humanity also shapes the word of God in the Gospels. So we take the Gospels as the Church's assured word of God despite the corrosive opinions of scholars who fear that, by their research, they have obliterated the historical humanity of Jesus of Nazareth.

They haven't. We may read the Gospels with a critical eye, but we read them with an open heart. The word of God is a living Word, and each time I turn to it with an open heart, I find there the living truth. I find there a human being who was born and grew up surrounded by other men and women, who worked and played, and who always did what the Father wanted done. Followers of Christ have discerned him—found him waiting—in the Scriptures for nearly two millennia. And we find this still true: "Those who accept his offer of salvation are set free from sin, sorrow, inner emptiness and loneliness."[83] This is the beginning of *The Joy of the Gospel.*

Then, second, we find Jesus Christ waiting for us in the Church, among the People of God. We encounter Jesus personally in belonging actively in the Church. This place usually includes the parents and siblings and relatives he gave to me. It includes the teachers I have had and the pastors. It is built on my race and language. This is the place where I could sing "Holy God" and feel like an angel. Belonging in the Church penetrates my city life and my work. When I find Jesus in this place, I find him waiting for me with open arms.

We may read the Gospels with a critical eye, but we read them with an open heart.

These "open arms" are not metaphorical. Jesus was quite explicit: *love one another; you must love one another just as I have loved you* (John 13:34, NJB). Our discerning work to shape a parish community goes deeper than good ecclesiology or good liturgy. It reaches obeying his commandment. It is bringing to our lifeworld the Mystical Body of Christ. It is where Jesus Christ personally encounters us.

Keeping mindful of his commandment alerts us to "a spiritual consumerism" offering a "disembodied Jesus who demands nothing of us with regard to others."[84] This is the individualism that turns the Jesus of the Gospels and the Church into a Savior I can be comfortable with. The "interest in spirituality today has to be discerned," certainly in the United States. Here, we are invited to a "spirituality of well-being" that is all about me even when it involves a community. We hear preached "theology of prosperity," deifying money and indifferent to responsibility for others.[85] Some embrace a Jesus of scented candles and a centering prayer that never gets outside the self. This is not the Jesus of the Gospels and the Church.

The third way we encounter Jesus, he told us himself: helping others in need. He was explicit: whatever we have done *to one of the least of these who are members of my family, you did it to me* (Matt. 25:40). Jesus chose to identify himself with the poor and needy. Reaching out to them is not for the sake of a good feeling and cheap grace. These "least" are a crowd of needy, hurt human beings—even the Syrian refugees—but especially the ones right around us. We are surrounded by people who need us. We cannot let our sophisticated consumerist culture complicate what is very simple.

The luminous incident of the Widow of Nain illustrates this encounter. Jesus told the weeping mother not to cry, and then he said, "Young man, I say to you, get up." As Carlo Martini pointed out, no word in Scripture is accidental and each of these counts.[86]

This young man, asleep in death, belongs to God's people. We wake up, most of us, and quite literally find ourselves belonging to the Church, though some of us are already adults when we are given the challenge of choosing.

Then his voice penetrates the sleep: "I say to you." Jesus addresses each of us. He knows our names. And when we turn to him in faith and hope, he will give us the name he means to call us, as he did when he called Simon "Peter, the rock." He says the same to us, calling us by the name he will use for us and giving us a mission. Or better, making us a mission, as Francis says of each of us: "I am a mission on this earth; that is the reason why I am here in this world."[87] We are salt for the earth and light for the world—the incarnate reign of Christ on earth.

And then Jesus said to the young man, *Get up*. We will not hear his voice unless we have grown into the contemplative mindset needed for discernment. That is our "getting up." The first sign of our openness to an encounter with Jesus Christ who is seeking us is reading the Gospels with an open heart.

18

Living Every Day in Christ

Christ's resurrection is not an event of the past; it contains a vital power which has permeated this world.
—Pope Francis

Jesus of Nazareth came from a small, rather despised town: *Can anything good come out of Nazareth?* (John 1:46). But he was born in a town with a name big in prophecies. Bethlehem was King David's city, and the prophet Micah, seven hundred years before Jesus' birth, prophesied something more: *O Bethlehem of Ephrathah . . . from you shall come forth for me one who is to rule in Israel, whose origin is from of old, from ancient days* (Mic. 5:2). Matthew tells us that this prophecy is fulfilled in Jesus, who was born in Bethlehem.

He was born there because Joseph belonged to the house of David and had to go register there. Joseph adopted Jesus as his own son. I've always liked the thought that Jesus was adopted, because I'm also adopted. We are those whom God *destined . . . for adoption as his children*, brothers and sisters of the Lord Jesus himself (Eph. 1:5).

Joseph was not a prince; he was a laboring man. In the natural course of his son's life, he brought Jesus to labor alongside him. Jesus had hands as hard as Joseph's. They both knew what payday meant, living from one to the next. This is history much more thoroughly testified to than the story of Socrates or Caesar.

Yet Jesus was the Son of God. Jesus soberly informed the learned scribes and priests, *the Father and I are one*, which shocked them (John 10:30). Making his real life even more mysterious, Jesus added that *the Father is in me and I am in the Father* (John 10:38). Pope Benedict XVI pointed out that Jesus was always in a union with the Father and the Spirit. He could not possibly not be, as we understand it, because the three divine Persons eternally live together as one God.

The person who knows how to discern recognizes that this is a mystery far, far beyond our grasp. Our minds are stuffed with science and media surveys, so that we see little difference between a problem and a mystery. We tend to feel that what cannot be solved by the human mind is not real. So when we think about the truth that Jesus Christ is both God and man, we really are challenged. The faith is a burden, Pope Francis once said. And the discerning mind recognizes that listening to the Word of God is a grace and that believing it with our hearts is a gift.

Without this gift, the human person cannot see beyond the surrounding horizon—that is, we cannot perceive life beyond death. When we accept, by the gift of faith, that Jesus Christ is God and Savior, we take into our hearts the hope that we belong to a humanity that will live forever. *As you therefore have received Christ Jesus the Lord, continue to live your lives in him, rooted and built up in him and established in the faith, just as you were taught, abounding in thanksgiving* (Col. 2:6–7).

Our minds are stuffed with science and media surveys, so that we see little difference between a problem and a mystery.

The deepest discernment about Jesus Christ is that he was born and lived for *me*; that he died and rose from the dead for *me*. We find this hard to comprehend, but we are already living in human flesh that is destined to live on into eternity. This is what Pope Francis was driving at: "Christ's resurrection is not an event of the past; it contains a vital power which has permeated this world."[88]

Why did Jesus come back in his own flesh? It was his flesh, indeed: the disciples could see and feel the wounds in his hands and side. What made Jesus come back in his flesh instead of as a glorified creature of awe and splendor?

He came back to show us what *our* future is: eternal life as our selves: enfleshed spirits or inspirited animals of flesh and blood. The discerning recognize that we now live in a humanity different from what it was before grace. *So for anyone who is in Christ, there is a new creation; the old order is gone and a new being is there to see* (2 Cor. 5:17, NJB).

This *new creation* affects every human being and it affects me. We see this happening all the time. When scientists learned how to vaccinate people for protection against hepatitis, measles, and polio, they protected whole cities and nations—and they protected *me*, personally. When the government mandated pure food, it defended everyone, and it defended *me*. When the local police stamp out crime, they make the city safer, and they make *me* safer.

In the same way, the Son of God's coming into human life opened the gate to eternal human life for everyone—and for *me*. When he embraced death and came out of it, he raised all humanity—and he raised *me*.

Mature disciples have prayed about this from the time they wrote down the first parts of the Gospels: the Passion narratives. This is how the second great discernment leads to a deep realization and acceptance of our human condition, torn as it is between disaster and delight, dark and light, suffering and joy.

Richard of Chichester left us his prayer: "Thanks be to Thee, Lord Jesus Christ, for all the benefits which thou hast given me, for all the pains and insults thou hast borne for me. O most merciful Redeemer, Friend, and Brother, may I know Thee more clearly, love Thee more dearly, and follow Thee more nearly, day by day." (He died in 1254.)

Note that knowing, loving, and following are not three successive stages in our life in Christ. They anchor the constant interplay of head, heart, and hands in the lives of those who have accepted life in Christ. They are faith, belief, and enactment done by creatures bound by time. We are already living Christ's resurrected life—but only day by day. Timelessly and entirely will come later, on the other side of the door of death.

Jesus did all this for *me*. I was unconscious of it, and perhaps uncaring even after I heard about it. How different my life becomes when I accept and embrace him. I was in God's mind, and the Son's, too, when he was born, died, and rose. And I am in God's mind, Father and Son and Spirit, now. And will be forever.

19

Growing in Wisdom, Age, and Grace

They were fully conscious of belonging to a large community which neither space nor time can limit.

—Pope Paul VI

Through distressing falls and disorienting blind alleys, we grow in wisdom and grace as well as in age. We learn. We are like Jesus in this: he had to learn.

He had to learn language to begin with, humbling himself as his brain stored words and the rules for combining them. He had an accent, Galilean like Peter's—*your accent gives you away*—the way our accents might give away our home in Fort Worth or Boston (Matt. 26:73, NJB).

His prayers sounded just like Joseph's because Joseph taught him to say them. If he built a chair, people would remark that "it's like Joseph used to make"; he was the carpenter's son. He was content with what the Father had prepared for him. This contentment grows only in deep humility, and *being found in human form, he humbled himself* (Phil. 2:7–8). It is the same for us: mature humility rests on accepting and enjoying the gifts of language, relations, and culture that God is giving us.

When Jesus was twelve, he mistakenly thought that the Father wanted him to learn the law and serve *in my Father's house*, the temple. His discerning parents thought otherwise. Joseph, whom the Lady Mary called *your father*, wanted him to stay home longer. So Jesus *went down with them and came to Nazareth*, where he obeyed them and *increased in wisdom and in years, and in divine and human favor*—or as we said for decades in the Douai version, *he grew in wisdom, age, and grace* (Luke 2:48–52).

As all parents must, the Lady Mary and Joseph of Nazareth watched their boy begin to make up his mind about what to do with his life. There were cultural pressures, of course, one of them being the question of whether he would marry or not. His cousin John was moving toward the life led by the ancient prophets. Jesus thought seriously about his cousin's way, as his fasting and prayer in the desert suggest. But he was deeply attracted by and attached to the revealed word of God—Jesus cites the Pentateuch, the prophets, and the Psalms a lot—and he came to appreciate his vocation to serve the Father by spreading the Good News among the people.

When it was time to start his public work, *he left Nazareth and made his home in Capernaum by the lake* (Matt. 4:13). He went to synagogue on Sabbath and sometimes taught. He paid the temple tax there. He cured Peter's mother-in-law of her fever and the centurion's little servant of his painful paralysis. He cured so many others in Capernaum that the people he grew up with in Nazareth grew jealous (see Luke 4:23). And sometimes there were so many guests in the house that the only way to get a sick man to him was through the roof.

Mature discernment draws us through the mystery of the universal Savior to encounter Jesus of Nazareth, the carpenter's son. What does his human life show us? To begin with, Jesus discerned the fullness of his vocation only slowly as his life unfolded. In his public life, he gathered seventy-two disciples who were willing to go to others and tell about the Good News. From among them, he chose twelve with whom he worked on "the challenge of finding and sharing a 'mystique' of living together, of mingling and encounter, of embracing and supporting one another."[89]

To begin with, Jesus discerned the fullness of his vocation only slowly as his life unfolded.

That is a challenge we know very well, even with our closest relations and friends. We are ferociously busy. We are hindered as much as helped by the panoply of electronic communications that not only connect us but also keep us apart. How can we get beyond the media's fixation on conflict, the cities' racial tensions, and our culture's obsession with sex? Even the maturely discerning struggle to see Christian life as "a genuine experience of fraternity, a caravan of solidarity, a sacred pilgrimage," as Francis thinks we can see it.[90]

We have to grow into this discernment, mastering prejudice, fear, and selfishness. To come to know him, we have to break through our culture's individualism. We are invited to yoga, centering prayer, "attentiveness," and "to escape from others and take refuge in the comfort of their privacy or in a small circle of close friends, renouncing the realism of the social aspect of the Gospel."[91] This is a very real temptation among Americans today as we build gated communities and stay in our dens, communicating on the Web, which we can turn off at will.

There is a parallel in Jesus' experience. At first, he felt and insisted that he had been sent *only to the lost sheep of the house of Israel* (Matt. 15:24). But when he experienced the Canaanites' and pagans' belief in him and his powers, he realized that *so must the Son of Man be lifted up, that whoever believes in him may have eternal life* (John 3:14–15). As he matured, Jesus came to grasp that the people's deepest enslavement was not to the Romans, just as ours is not to taxes or the economy or government regulations. Jesus heard Nehemiah's lament: *Here we are, slaves to this day—slaves in the land that you gave to our ancestors to enjoy its fruit and its good gifts* (Neh. 9:36). But Jesus saw beyond that political servitude. The people were slaves to a self-centered uprightness that let them ignore their neighbors.

Jesus' life will always present to us "a summons to overcome suspicion, habitual mistrust, fear of losing our privacy, all the defensive attitudes which today's world imposes on us."[92] We might hear wise secular advice in this. But Pope Francis continues and goes beyond that: "True faith in the incarnate Son of God is inseparable from self-giving, from membership in the community, from service, from reconciliation with others."

As we mature in discernment, we go beyond loving only family and friends. We reach out, learning first to be civil and affable to strangers. But we are urgently invited to go still further and love those who hate you, do good to those who hurt you (see Matt. 5:44). We learn to think of "them" not as a crowd of strangers and odd foreigners but as the many individual persons for whom Jesus cares.

And we grow beyond a narrow view of what parish is, or diocese, or even national church. Discerning love will help us grow to be "fully conscious of belonging to a large community which neither space nor time can limit."[93] And in it, we wait joyfully for his second coming.

20

Discernment Teaches and Forms Us through Suffering

In the cross is the history of the world: grace and sin, mercy and repentance, good and evil, time and eternity.
—Pope Francis

Trying to express a profound mystery, the letter to the Hebrews paints the frame: *during his life on the earth*, Jesus faced bitter suffering that was unjust and deeply insulting. He prayed most earnestly *with loud cries and with tears* to his Father, *who had the power to save him from death* (Heb. 5:7, NJB). In words every child has learned, he begged, *Father, if you are willing, remove this cup from me; yet, not my will but yours be done* (Luke 22:42). Then, in a paradox that hides the deep mystery of sin and suffering, Jesus *learnt obedience* (Heb. 5:8, NJB).

This is the first thing a disciple of Christ learns about sin and suffering: "In the cross is the history of the world: grace and sin, mercy and repentance, good and evil, time and eternity."[94] We will never understand this because suffering is not just a fact in our experience; suffering is an evil and a mystery. We do know that humankind was meant not to suffer but to live in a garden of joy. Instead, we sinned and did evil. In every suffering is some kind of evil, so when we suffer, we are putting up with evil in patience, as God in eternity puts up with evil in patience.

But our faith tells more about human suffering than that we imitate God when we bear it patiently. The faith tells us that Jesus Christ accepted suffering for our sakes. We are blinded by the mystery of iniquity, but with prayer, we can come to see that, really and truly, *he was wounded for our transgressions, crushed for our iniquities; upon him was the punishment that made us whole, and by his bruises we are healed* (Isa. 53:5).

So in the *Spiritual Exercises,* Ignatius suggests that we pray "for sorrow, compassion, and shame because the Lord is going to His suffering *for my sins.*"[95] He will be tortured viciously and fixed to a cross to hang in agony to the end. But his spirit finds no other exit—no other *exodus* and no other *Passover*. This is how, *Son though he was, thorough his suffering* he became *for all who obey him, the source of eternal salvation* (Heb. 5:8–9). Here is the truth: for each of us who obey him, Jesus suffered for *me*.

With prayer, we can go even beyond this in our discernment. For our faith reveals to us that when we suffer, we are suffering *with* Jesus. This discernment is a further step. Ignatius signals that by suggesting as prayer on Jesus' Passion continues, that "it is proper to ask for sorrow *with* Christ in sorrow, anguish *with* Christ in anguish."[96]

• • •

Our faith teaches us that we are his Mystical Body: *Ours were the sufferings he was bearing, ours the sorrows he was carrying* (Isa. 53:4, NJB). His acceptance of the sufferings inflicted on him is our acceptance of the sufferings inflicted on us. As he learned obedience through suffering, we learn obedience through suffering. As he was humiliated by pain, we are humiliated by pain. When we stand with loved ones who suffer, in Pope Francis's experience, we can rightly feel that we are "touching the suffering flesh of Christ in others."[97]

With prayer, we can come to believe in our hearts—even when we are going through a long bout of breast cancer or prostate cancer—what apostle Paul felt: *in my flesh I am completing what is lacking in Christ's afflictions for the sake of his body, that is, the church* (Col. 1:24). Mature disciples can come to contentment in the thought that the battle for humankind continues. We are his Mystical Body; we are the beginning of resurrected life on earth. If we are persecuted and pummeled by the consequences of sin, we can accept it into our own persons as completing Christ's saving act.

In all of this, we have to have the great virtue that he had: hope. He had to learn hope; we have to learn hope. It is not cheap. Jesus of Nazareth had to hope that what he had gotten himself into did, indeed, fulfill the prophecies of the suffering servant: *See, my servant shall prosper; he shall be exalted and lifted up, and shall be very high* (Isa. 52:13). The irony of that "lifted very high" drove Jesus to the next verses: *he was despised and rejected . . . a man of suffering . . . held of no account* (KJV): useless, purposeless, inane.

Every disciple who has faced bitter illness, harsh suffering, and approaching death has this same experience of feeling useless, purposeless, inane. Questions press in on us: Why *me*? What sense does this make? For as Pope Francis has pointed out, suffering is personal and cannot be shared. Others can be compassionate, but they cannot take my suffering from me; it is mine. Now I know that as Jesus' suffering was his, so my suffering is mine. I take it as he took his.

Jesus of Nazareth had to hope that what he had gotten himself into did, indeed, fulfill the prophecies of the suffering servant.

I have watched by the prolonged deathbed struggle of more than one Jesuit. One who died just weeks before I wrote this had lain paralyzed and immobile for more than a year. He shared with me that he sometimes felt empty and hopeless and like a cipher. When he did, he would turn immediately to prayers stored in his memory—just as Jesus did on his cross. I learned myself the precious value of memorized prayers and psalms and hymns when the hours of the night are long and lonely: *they nourish patience*. This paralytic Jesuit was never impatient and reached out to whoever came into his room even when the effort was almost visible.

That we use drugs to take the edges off of physical decay does not relieve us of having to hope that good will come to us, or free us of temptations to rage and despair. Serious pain—it's in the "hands" part of the discernment cycle, the "what we do"—can mess up our thoughts and completely wipe out any other feelings. We feel impulsively that "I've got to get out of here" as pain becomes a stark solitary confinement. We are correct to alleviate serious pain. But even while doing it, we are also very correct to join ourselves to Jesus in his zone and in his trust of the Father.

Or zones, rather, for we are baptized into his resurrection as well as into his death. *For if we have been united with him in a death like his, we will certainly be united with him in a resurrection like his* (Rom. 6:5). Even through morphine, the discerning person holds on to that hard, stern hope—a fierce kind of joy. *We know that our old self was crucified with him so that the body of sin might be destroyed, and we might no longer be enslaved to sin.* Holding on to Jesus Christ, we pull out of dark despair, however long the suffering might last. We believe, and enact that belief in calm acceptance. Because *if we have died with Christ, we believe that we will also live with him* (Rom. 6:6, 8).

21

Discernment Guides Us to Forgive as Jesus Forgave

The Church must be a place of mercy freely given, where everyone can feel welcomed, loved, forgiven and encouraged to live the good life of the Gospel.
—Pope Francis

Not long after she began a retreat at a house in the East, a woman came to talk with me about the rancor in her heart. She was (understandably) angry that her spouse had cheated on her. Not "all the way," she said, but he was in love with his secretary, and that hurt his wife. She was in an ugly mood.

I didn't see her again until after I had talked about forgiveness and reconciliation and how we needed to imitate Jesus of Nazareth. We have to do what we say in the Our Father: "as we forgive those who trespass against us." The morning after that, she came in again. She was not in the ugly mood. Neither was she entirely happy with herself and her spouse. But what Nelson Mandela had said—I'd quoted him the evening before—struck her as sensible: holding a resentment against someone is like putting poison in your tea expecting it to hurt the other person. She began working to forgive as Jesus forgave.

Here's how Jesus forgave, at least as I see it.

- First, he knew the injury done him: they were nailing him to the cross.
- Second, he asked the Father to forgive the men doing this—so of course Jesus had forgiven them. He had taught us to pray, "forgive us our trespasses as we forgive those who trespass against us." So when Jesus asked the Father to forgive the men, Jesus had already done it.
- Third, astonishingly, Jesus gave the Father a reason to forgive them:

for they know not what they are doing. Of course, the Father already knew that. So why was Jesus saying it? Perhaps because Jesus needed to say it, out loud, to make it real.

- Finally, all along, Jesus was praying for those who were murdering him. From the beginning of the brutal, inhuman hurt being done him, Jesus was praying not for himself but for them.

Forgiving as Jesus forgave, we pray for those who harm and hurt us: Give them eternal life, Lord, and give them all good things now. You cannot beg God to give all good things to a person you resent and reject. I find that we have to work at this third step. We have to wonder how they could have done what they did to us. What was in their experience that prepared them to act this way—whether guiltily or only half aware? Unless we come to empathize with our violators, even eventually feel compassion for them, we may forgive them, but we will not know that we have. Not in our heart of hearts. I think that this is the desolation St. Ignatius mentions that "leads to a lack of confidence" and brings us to live "without hope, without love." How can we be confident we have forgiven?

You cannot beg God to give all good things to a person you resent and reject.

I was given a beautiful story about this. I had come to know an elegant black woman in spiritual direction. I'll call her Lily because she was as beautiful as that. She had been abused as a girl by her father, all during the long years of her girlhood. She had chosen to forgive him for what he did, and she prayed for him when he died. But she had a nagging fear that she hadn't really forgiven him.

I wondered at first if Lily's dilemma was the victim mentality our current culture promotes—that is, to live with the feeling that our hurts are permanent and we are helpless against them. But that was not true of Lily. She felt that she had gotten over her anger and resentment; she had truly forgiven her father and was not clinging to being a victim. What she was experiencing was subtler than that: an evil spirit, pushing her to suffer a "lack of confidence" that God had accepted her forgiveness. That fretfulness kept her feeling aware of the abuse she had suffered. God forgets our sins; Satan will not and wants us not to.

When I first met Lily, her deep feeling of regret had lasted so long that she really had lost hope that she could live tranquil and content in this matter. Moreover, she had not been able to feel love; she had tried two marriages and failed. She was actually being tempted to believe that she could not belong to the Church that was "a place of mercy freely given, where everyone can feel welcomed, loved, forgiven and encouraged to live the good life of the Gospel."[98]

How can we forgive the harm others have done to us? What they have done is wrong and sinful. We can recognize that. We can also recognize that we are sinful too and, with compassion like the Father's, try to understand what in them or in their experience allowed them to harm us, or even drove them to harm us.

In this vein, Lily remembered some facts about her father's very harsh and deprived boyhood—how he had, himself, been severely abused in ways I won't go into here. She remembered that he had been ignored and despised by his own father, her grandfather. He had been sent to wretchedly poor schools where he learned little but wrong behavior. In all of her father's miserable wrong, this elegant woman found she could offer to God the Father not reasons her father should have abused her, but reasons God the Father could forgive him for what he did.

Then she found that she had, indeed, forgiven him. She knew it now and found consolation. She gladly belongs in the Church of mercy.

Forgiveness—and forgiven-ness—are at the heart of Christian experience: when we forgive, we grasp how we are forgiven, ourselves. We cherish the same love that the Holy Spirit confirmed in Jesus of Nazareth, who forgave even his enemies. Forgiven ourselves, we forgive others, even our enemies, even those who hate us. One of the deepest wellsprings of desolate lives in our day is the refusal to forgive—the need to have revenge, to sue, and to get back at people. It's desolation, pure and simple. Poison in your own tea.

Touchstones

- The second great discernment: Jesus is the universal Savior, and he is the Savior for me.
- Jesus of Nazareth is the image of the unseen God and shows us what God is like.
- Jesus chose us; we did not choose him. And he sent us to bring his reign, a new Christian humanism, to the world.
- We encounter Jesus, personally, in loving one another and in helping those in need.
- Jesus learned what he was to do as his vocation in life unfolded.
- Mature Christians come to grasp that we live and move in human flesh now summoned through the ongoing resurrection into eternal life.
- Yet in this life, we are filling up with our sufferings Christ's sufferings for his Church.
- The cross shows the full reality of our human story: sin and grace, love and hate, death and life.
- The mature disciple learns to forgive as Jesus forgave. Jesus Christ's Church is the Church of mercy.

Christ's Fire and Light

As dark falls on Holy Saturday, Catholics gather in front of their parish churches. The pastor builds a new fire. From it, we light the Easter candle—the splendid symbol of Christ, the light of the world. Then we process into the church, singing "Christ Our Light." The deacon carries the Easter candle, and each person in the congregation lights his or her light from the Christ candle.

See this, now: as each of us lights our own candles from that one Easter candle, it loses nothing. It flames just as steadily, as though no one were touching it. It's the way the living Jesus of Nazareth was steady and sure when the woman with a bloody flux touched him and was healed by his power. He felt it go out to her, but he did not lose anything at all.

It's the same with the Easter candle. As each of us takes flame from it, it burns steady and sure. Yet each of our candles takes fire from it. Here is an excellent symbol of our living in Christ. He lives still, in our flesh and in God, and he gives us life. Now each of us lives our own lives—yet that life is Christ's, from which we receive our life.

St. Paul reminded the Romans of Isaiah's prophecy: *from him and through him and to him are all things* (Rom. 10:36). As all the light in the church on Holy Saturday comes from the Easter candle, so all our lives come from God. And yet God loses nothing; like the candle, he is steady and sure. God creates us and shares with us, and we are correct to love our own living and being, enlightened by the lights around us.

PART FIVE

THE HOLY SPIRIT AT WORK AMONG US

22

The Spirit and Discernment in the World

Seeing reality with the eyes of faith, we cannot fail to acknowledge what the Holy Spirit is sowing.

—Pope Francis

The Spirit we receive at baptism brings us *life in union with Christ Jesus* (Rom. 8:1). The Spirit also endows each of us with "the sense of faith, which is a gift that the Spirit gives to all the faithful."[99] That gift gives us "a certain connaturality with divine realities, and a wisdom which enables them to grasp those realities intuitively."[100]

These "divine realities" reach beyond abstruse theological points and dogmas because "Christian doctrine is not a closed system, incapable of raising questions, doubts, inquiries, but is living, is able to unsettle, is able to enliven."[101] These divine realities reach into prayer, worship, feeding the hungry, and housing the homeless. They have to do with the Church being a "battlefield hospital." Among these divine realities, almost invisible to most of us, is what Pope Francis calls "this daily sanctity."[102] But they have to do even with the national affairs of our country—especially with how we perceive and acknowledge God in America.

If we are not discerning at some considerable depth, we will unthinkingly adopt what the "talking class"—Bill O'Reilly (FOX); Rachel Maddow (MSNBC); Anderson Cooper (CNN); Diane Sawyer (ABC); Wolf Blitzer (CNN)—believes about God in America. In their reports, catastrophe, tragedy, and public immorality pop up every day. The huge majority of reports on the Catholic Church—before Pope Francis began making the news—had to do with the evil behavior of 2 percent of Catholic priests.

These commentators make you wonder whether they agree with Sigmund Freud's judgments that America is a grandiose experiment but a gigantic mistake that will not succeed.

So with the eyes of faith, we ask, What is the Holy Spirit "sowing" in our nation now that "we cannot fail to acknowledge?"[103] The answer of a group of men making a retreat together in Grand Coteau was to sing "America the Beautiful" at Mass. Their *sensus fidei* helped them see that our culture has a current of faith in God as deep as the Grand Canyon. They know the truth of what Pope Francis observed: "An evangelized popular culture contains values of faith and solidarity capable of encouraging the development of a more just and believing society, and possesses a particular wisdom which ought to be gratefully acknowledged."[104]

The mature disciple will note that the Spirit empowers us, not to do what Freud thought he could do and judge America's future, but to appreciate America's present for the good God pours out on us. Appreciating our own culture is not patriotism or jingoism. Our appreciation for our own culture is an important aspect of mature discernment, because gratitude must ground the mature disciples' "unique and irreplaceable contribution to the elaboration of an authentic evangelical discernment in the various situations and cultures in which men and women live."[105]

So with the eyes of faith, we ask, What is the Holy Spirit "sowing" in our nation now that "we cannot fail to acknowledge?"

Think of these present realities to make this "authentic evangelical discernment." In the face of reported decline in belief, most members of the 114th Congress identify not as unbelievers or religious "none's," but as Christians. The Pew Research Center reports that about one in three members of the 114th Congress identify as Roman Catholic, though Catholics make up little more than one-fifth of the whole population (69 Republicans and 68 Democrats among the 435 House members).[106] Maybe the pope's prayer for more good politicians is being answered—if only they could get their act together.

But let's look beyond the politicians to see what the Spirit is doing out in the general population. A recent report noted that of all Americans getting health care, one in six finds it in Catholic institutions. Hundreds of hospitals were quietly opened by religious women in every corner of the country. Another study estimated that one out of every five Americans living in poverty is served by Catholics, and a great number of these are served in their parishes. The Church resettles the largest number of refugees of any agency in the country, and St. Vincent de Paul serves fourteen million needy persons every year. Overseas, the Catholic Relief Services addresses the needs of nearly 100 million people in ninety-three countries—without a lot of noise or notice. While the press focused on the abuse of the young, the Catholic Church has kept educating the young. We are the largest private educator in the nation. In 2010, two million students were enrolled in 6,890 K–12 Catholic schools. Even with lots of statistical qualifiers, the Catholic Church proves to be the most important nongovernmental source of social service in the nation.

The discerning disciple understands that to take note of these realities does not make you vain or a braggart; it forms the necessary ground for gratitude. Seen from the Spirit's viewpoint, the real situation of our culture in which Christian men and women live inspires hope. The Spirit sees our penchant for violence and our inveterate racism, of course. But the Spirit has also been sowing deep in America's soul a strong belief in God and Jesus Christ. Each of us needs to observe and also profess this deep layer of religion in the American character. The agnostic would prefer us to think that the religious spirit that once thrived like the grain fields in the Midwest is now blown away like the deserts in the West. We are very wise to reject this assessment. It will affect our discernments.

The Spirit moves when and where the Spirit wills. We live the conviction that the Holy Spirit is giving us wisdom, understanding, and knowledge about the next good thing we are to do. This means that the Holy Spirit is currently "sowing" these things among us, and we are not very discerning if we do not expect to experience them. Each of us is responsible to read the signs of our own times in our own lifeworld of family and friends, of work and leisure, and to heed the Spirit. Then we can become salt for our place and light for our time. This is what Pope Francis means when he writes: "*I am a mission* on this earth; that is the reason why I am here in this world."[107] And Americans are privileged to live "this daily sanctity."

23

The Spirit of an Acting God

The memory of the past accompanies us not as a dead weight but as a reality interpreted in the light of our present consciousness.

—Pope Francis

I stood one day on the cliff above the Columbia River where it runs into Portland, and I watched the muscular river driving toward the sea. A child would probably not wonder where the river comes from; the river simply is. But like any adult, I wondered. I knew that this great river does not invent itself. It rises in a source, a source that continually works and pours out water. I stood delighted by the splendid scene, my delight not diminished by the knowledge that the river has a source—or rather, sources.

I think Pope Francis was driving at this concept when he told his Jesuit friends, "Ours is not a 'lab faith,' but a 'journey faith,' a historical faith. God has revealed himself as history, not as a compendium of abstract truths."[108] The pope had written earlier that as a consequence of this journey faith, "The memory of the past accompanies us not as a dead weight but as a reality interpreted in the light of our present consciousness."[109] This idea takes some unpacking.

When a child, I hardly wondered where I came from. Now, as a grown man, I do well to consider that I am not my own source, not at my conception or my birth or at any moment of my life. I am sourced in every action, all my life long, as the rivers are: steadily, through their whole length. I am constantly summoned into life and light by Another.

This does not mean that I am not free to make something of myself or to ruin my own life if I choose to. Being sourced, I am not in the iron grip of fate. It's all right to believe in good luck or random chance. I don't believe in them; I *experience* them. But we have considered that within, behind, and before them lies the One who reveals himself in all that happens.

Early one morning during a thorny patch in my year, I was going to the chapel. Out of my early-morning dimness, I asked the Holy Spirit for her blessing. She gave me confidence in that moment in what we say all the time (often in moments of distress or self-blame): "God likes us the way we are because God is making us the way we are."

This is not philosophy or theology. It is a faith-filled observation on our personal story, because our faith means believing in the history of The People and in our own personal history of coming to belong among them. The mature will recognize that we are person as God is person—always with the others.

My parents wanted a child. They could not have wanted *me* because I did not yet exist. But God wanted me. My parents could not have decided whether their child would be boy or girl. But they did decide to offer me to the Lord and have me baptized.

From that instant, I was not merely the latest model of a bucket of mud with human DNA. I was also the youngest sibling of Jesus Christ. I became a living member of his Mystical Body. I belonged to his Church. All of that my Creator and Lord wanted in me.

As everyone's does, my life story begins to weave among feelings and convictions that I am to cherish or to reject. I grow aware of actions that I am to do or keep from doing. All this goes on whether I like it or not, and even whether I am willing or not. Thus, I am to honor in my heart and deeds my father and mother. I am to fit in with brother and sister, meld myself into cousins and uncles and aunts, expand into friendships and fence with unfriendly others. Always, my story flows through those I am to love, put into my life by my Father, the love rising steadily out of the Holy Spirit of Love.

All along, the Holy Spirit goes on shaping me for the mission the Father hopes I will fulfill. The younger we are, the less shaped we are. Our brains are filled with cells waiting to be linked with others. The older we grow, the more the neural connections are linked into patterns. But the Holy Spirit can and does move in us at every age. An uncle of mine went through a case of beer every weekend, his brain firmly patterned. He asked the Holy Spirit to help him quit. When he was well up in years, he did quit. No withdrawal, no struggle. He just quit. He was puzzled that it came so easy. And he was quite sure the Holy Spirit had answered his prayer. I agreed with him.

> All along, the Holy Spirit goes on shaping me for the mission the Father hopes I will fulfill.

I am free to offer to the Lord God this homage: joy in my rising this day, joy in my limbs and my body's appetites, joy in the next good thing to do. This homage I offer God—I know that I am bound to do and to avoid, to embrace and to reject, to love some things and acts and to hate others. This is homage: knowing that I did not design these things for myself but God did—not just this earthly, passing moment but in his eternal *Now*. And I say yes.

For the Son of God, Jesus Christ, in whose likeness we are being shaped, *was not "Yes and No"; but in him it is always "Yes."* We pray to be like him with great heart and generous spirit. *For this reason it is through him that we say the "Amen," to the glory of God* (2 Cor. 1:19–20).

24

The Holy Spirit and the Prayer of Consideration

I pray mentally even when I am waiting at the dentist or at other times of the day.
—Pope Francis

Mature discernment grows only with mental prayer. This is prayer beyond liturgical worship, formulas such as the rosary, or petitionary prayers asking God for something or asking a saint for help. Mental prayer means taking time to be mindful of God's loving presence and aware of his creating action—and then thinking, wondering, and desiring, and perhaps also listening to and talking with God.

Mental prayer is the usual means by which the Spirit draws us to ongoing conversion of mind and heart. It is where we change attitudes and sort out what we want. Mental prayer helps mature disciples go about doing what St. Paul told the Romans to do: *let the renewing of your minds transform you, so that you may discern for yourselves what is the will of God—what is good and acceptable and mature.*[110]

This "renewing of mind" that will transform us comes only with prayer. A lot of us are being led to prayer by movements full of the Spirit, such as Bible study, Cursillo, Christ Renews His Parish, Legionaries, or Couples for Christ. We find resources on the Web, too. The manager of a big law firm in Dallas opens her day with fifteen minutes of prayer guided by a website created by young Jesuit seminarians.[111]

This "renewing of mind" that will transform us comes only with prayer.

Many followers of Christ begin or end their day with the readings assigned to the liturgy of the day. They adopt the ancient practice of *Lectio Divina*. They read the passage, note words and phrases that strike them, and then take a little while to meditate on what they noted. The Gospels and the apostolic letters are the unique source of this renewing of mind and heart. Pope Francis points out that conversion of heart to God "is based on that word, listened to, meditated upon, lived, celebrated and witnessed to."[112]

Texts and websites can help mental prayer. But mental prayer is fundamentally an act of the individual. It must begin with silence and quiet—both. Silence happens outside us when people are not talking and our cell phones and televisions are turned off. Quiet is inside us, in a heart and mind unafraid of being alone and wakeful. St. Catherine of Siena wrote that every one of us has a little room in our heart where only "I and God" can ever go. When we sit in silence and go quietly into that little room, we find God already there. As Jesus said: *Those who love me will keep my word, and my Father will love them, and we will come to them and make our home with them* (John 14:23).

Every mature Christian can learn how to pray mentally. The gifts of faith, hope, and love make praying as natural to us as breathing is—if only we take the time. And every one of us prays in his or her unique way. A very successful company owner began his day with the classic Morning Offering. Over the years, he said, he found himself repeating parts of it during the day. Gradually, the time he took to pray in the morning got longer. Well before he retired, he realized that he was even praying while waiting for a client or in his car at a red light, "working things out with the Lord."

He had stumbled into the kind of prayer that comes most readily to us who live in the busyness of everyday life. "Working things out with the Lord" is the prayer of consideration, a true prayer though not often recognized as such. It is not new. Jesus did it. Think of what he was doing when he spent the night in prayer before choosing the Twelve. A wise and prudent man, he was considering in the Father's presence who among the seventy-two are *those whom you gave me* (John 17:9). He was "working out" with the Father and the Spirit whom he would make the special twelve disciples.

Jesus taught the Our Father once; he taught the prayer of consideration over and over again and showed us how to do it. He told the disciples to *consider the lilies of the field*, how the Father designs them and waters them, more beautiful than Solomon's robes, and consider that we mean more to the Father than lilies ever can (Matt. 6:28). He urged them to consider prayerfully being ready for life that will endure eternally instead of fretting about making money before you die, because *wherever your treasure is, there will your heart be too* (Matt. 6:21, NJB).

And think of the Sermon on the Mount. They say it's a sin to murder. I say, consider it a sin to call someone a fool. They say it's a sin to have sex with another's spouse. I say, consider it a sin to want to do so in your heart. Other gods teach hatred of enemies; consider what it means that God our Father pours out his sun and rain on enemies as well as friends. So Jesus figured out this principle: *set no bounds to your love, just as your heavenly Father sets none to his.*[113] Instead, let your compassion pour out into everyone in your everyday life.

Jesus' plain call on the prayer of consideration did one crucial thing: it kept him from focusing on himself. Prayer today seems to lead to that: "centering" is good, but what comes next? "There is always the risk that some moments of prayer can become an excuse for not offering one's life in mission; a privatized lifestyle can lead Christians to take refuge in some false forms of spirituality."[114]

Mental prayer outside of convents and monasteries means taking our day with us into mindfulness of God. He is always with us, going through things with us. In him, we can think about whatever we need to think about: a hard or disappearing job, a stressed spouse, a needy neighbor, a car to fix or replace. And we can do this any time of the day, "even when I am waiting at the dentist" or any other pleasant venue.[115] For God is creating us to thrive in the tangle of our minds and the welter of our emotions.

Consideration is the prayer of the mother of a teen-aged daughter. Her faith is that God calls this splendid child to life through her body and heart.

What weight shall she give to doubts about the daughter's steady date? What saying of Jesus does she need to recall right now? As she considers this in God's presence, she is praying mentally—and discerning. God loves to be with us when we do all of this, even when—we can say with the pope—"even when I get distracted and think of other things, or even fall asleep praying."[116] Well, well; consider that.

25

The Holy Spirit and Fear of the Lord

Through fear of the Lord, "we become, as Jesus asks us, like little children, trusting in the goodness and the protection of our heavenly Father. The Spirit enables us to persevere in loving obedience to the word of God."
—Pope Francis

The book of Proverbs sets out to help the simple and the young. But it admits right up front that those of us who have reached maturity should *listen and learn yet more* and that *a person of discernment will acquire the art of guidance* (Prov. 1:5). In that secret of discernment lies wrapped our "image of God"—that is, who God is in truth and who God is for me.

We know God differently as we grow in discernment and in discipline. Characteristically, the young and simple appreciate God as all-loving and gentle. One instructor in a seminar on spirituality shared a list of "Images of God" that began with "Gentle One" and ran through "Compassionate One," "Tender One," "Comforter," to "God of Dreams" and "Mystery of Love." Only one of some thirty images mentioned justice, and its point was that God is tender with the powerless.

The God in these images was the One who comes to the young and tender-minded. But so great is his mercy that God comes in just such guises to any of us when we are distraught by failures or dismayed by injustices. For "God's infinite power does not lead us to flee his fatherly tenderness, because in him affection and strength are joined."[117] By and large, everyone alive does well to know God as the Compassionate One, the Comforter, and the Mystery of Love. This is the God Francis proclaimed in the first words of his opening homily as Bishop of Rome: "What a beautiful truth of faith this is for our lives: the mercy of God!"[118]

As we mature in our faith, however, we *listen and learn yet more* because we grow more and more open to the Spirit's multiplicity of gifts. Principally in our failures, we grow aware that God is not only mercy and love; God is also holiness and justice. Then we exercise the gift of the Holy Spirit we call "fear of the Lord." With this gift, we have a mind and heart "like little children, trusting in the goodness and the protection of our heavenly Father."[119] At the same time, we know that *God sees us for what we are* (2 Cor. 5:11, NJB). We might have good reason to feel terrified, particularly when we have really hurt another. *For judgment will be without mercy to anyone who has shown no mercy*, St. James wrote (James 2:13).

But then he immediately adds that *mercy triumphs over judgment*. Hence, *with the fear of the Lord always in mind*, the mature disciple appreciates how utterly God knows us, every fiber of body and every breath of soul, and how entirely God's love sponges out our sins. Only the evil one knows God and is known by God and is terrified. When the holy turn to God, we are filled with wonder and awe. This wonder and awe is the Holy Spirit's gift of "fear of the Lord."

When the holy turn to God, we are filled with wonder and awe. This wonder and awe is the Holy Spirit's gift of "fear of the Lord."

• • •

Once I have accepted the Spirit's leading and discerned that God is my own Creator and Lord, my sins and failures are focused in this new frame: *his mercy is for those who fear him from generation to generation* (Luke 1:50). I fear the Lord, but not with a fear like that of a city boy lost all night in a wilderness. It is the fear of the lad who had not memorized the psalm his class was assigned to recite. When his turn came, he recited fearlessly: "The Lord is my Shepherd, and that's all I need to know."

Mature followers of Jesus are led by the Spirit to the holy fear of the Lord, for "God's infinite power does not lead us to flee his fatherly tenderness, because in him affection and strength are joined,"[120] God's faithful love is the source of my being, and I return that love.

Yet I have reason to fear my own self. I am an ordinary man or woman among ordinary men and women, and I commit actual sins and have to beg God's forgiveness. And the mature know the truth of what Pope Francis claims: "Only someone who has encountered mercy, who has been caressed by the tenderness of mercy, is happy and comfortable with the Lord."[121]

Being "happy and comfortable with the Lord" seems to have come very easily to some of the saints. Think of the innocent Thérèse of Lisieux or the deeply courageous Damien the Leper or the bold Maximilian Kolbe. To them, holiness of life and comfort with the Lord seemed almost a destiny. But most of us, even those whose lives have come to radiate holiness, have to struggle through failures before becoming comfortable with the Lord. Through the sacrament of reconciliation, "The Spirit enables us to persevere in loving obedience to the word of God."[122]

This explains why the Church is shifting its focus from the truths of the faith to the hope of our salvation. During the decades before Vatican II, the Church of Rome clung to a fear of God coming to judge the living and the dead that bordered on holy terror. Our great-grandparents really did hear thunderous sermons rolling through a catalogue of sins that made them all liable to hell. God the Righteous Judge would welcome the sheep into his kingdom, but definitely not the goats.

Yet even burdened with this vivid image of God's revenge, Catholics lived by a miracle of grace a life of deep faith and vibrant hope, little children, trusting in the goodness and the protection of our heavenly Father.[123] I remember distinctly hearing thunderous sermons when I was a boy and was allowed to attend "men's night" with my father. The catalogue of sins was long and the punishment dire, and the first time I went, I held my father's hand all the way home. But I learned how my father and mother and our Catholic neighbors lived. They proved Hilaire Belloc correct:

> Wherever the Catholic sun doth shine,
> there's always laughter and good red wine.
> At least, I've always found it so.
> Benedicamus Domino!

This is how the mature disciple goes along discerning the next good thing to do and leaving the future in God's hands. *Benedicamus Domino!* Why not?

26

Discerning Vocation and Mission

We can "thwart" God's dream if we fail to let ourselves be guided by the Holy Spirit.[124]

—Pope Francis

About discerning our call or vocation, the first thing to say is that we all share in the greatest one. God "calls humankind to seek him, to know him, and to love him with all our strength."[125] This is God's call to all, and it tells about God's dream: an earth peopled with lovers—with those who let the Holy Spirit lead them to love God, love one another, and love themselves—passionately and well.

How is humankind responding? Well, a look at history might be discouraging. Americans killed more Americans in our Civil War than foreign enemies killed in all other wars together. And look at international news now. You won't find many nice stories. Look around and see how badly we have thwarted God's dream. Humanity tends not to follow the Holy Spirit of love but instead leans into a spirit of darkness. Yet God remains faithful, patiently pursuing his project.

This is why the Son came into our flesh: to call us back into God's dream. Our faith tells us that this call somehow resonates in every human alive. This is what Jesus said: *And I, when I am lifted up from the earth, will draw all people to myself* (John 12:32). Everyone has to discern this great call; and that's the first thing to say about discerning our vocation in life.

The second thing to say about discerning our vocation is that we who have accepted Jesus as Lord now *live our lives in him, rooted in him and built up on him, held firm by the faith* (Col. 2:6–7, NJB). When we enact our belief in him, we make up the living Mystical Body of Christ. Now, St. Peter wrote, *you are a chosen race, a royal priesthood, a holy nation, God's own people* (1 Pet. 2:9).

This is why the Son came into our flesh: to call us back into God's dream. Our faith tells us that this call somehow resonates in every human alive.

Notice that our call to live in Christ is not a private matter—it's not "just about me." We belong to Christ's people, and it is crucial to realize that "without this sense of belonging we cannot understand our deepest identity."[126] This mentality of belonging can be difficult for those of us who live in individualistic cultures, in which we are told that a person can be authentic only when he or she has created a deep, personal identity. But this is a dangerous assumption. I have observed that the way into disbelief often begins when a person tries to travel solo.

When we live as discerning disciples, we call to mind that we are in God's image and thus always related to others. Belonging to Christ's people is not "just a part of my life or a badge I can take off; it is not an 'extra' or just another moment in life."[127] The truly discerning discover that the more deeply each one becomes himself or herself, the more we turn out to be deeply like one another.

There is another reason our vocation in Christ is not about us only as individuals. "All the baptized, whatever their position in the Church or their level of instruction in the faith, are agents of evangelization."[128] Being an evangelizer does not mean that each of us is called to teach or preach or proselytize. To begin with, Francis says, "It is not by proselytizing that the Church grows, but 'by attraction.'"[129]

What attraction? The attraction of a people "who wish to share their joy, who point to a horizon of beauty, and who invite others to a delicious banquet."[130] We show just by living a Christian life that God is love and Jesus brought us joy. As Francis puts it, "the essential vocation and mission of the lay faithful is to strive that earthly realities and all human activity may be transformed by the Gospel."[131] If I live a joyful life and everyone can tell that I've got this "thing" for God and obviously believe that tomorrow's going to be just splendid, I am living my vocation.

Here's the word: we are *witnesses.* American Catholics hesitate to witness to our faith. Perhaps we dread sounding like fundamentalists. Perhaps, too, we still face pockets of anti-Catholicism. Then there are the secular media: television, newspapers, the Web, magazines. Most reporters are agnostic or atheist and no more objective in their thinking than any of us. But they get to broadcast their prejudices. The media insist that the nation is inexorably growing secular, unreligious—even irreligious. I don't believe that. I believe that our civil order is getting more secular (separation and all that), but as a people we remain religious. Further, we Catholics and all sound Christians are a secure redoubt against that erosion. All we are called to do is to be discerning selves, authentically and transparently.

• • •

Each of us has a personal vocation—a mission from God into our time and place. So the third thing to say about vocation concerns what the word used to mean: a vocation to be married or celibate, lay or religious. St. Paul's personal opinion was that Christians are called to marriage. But this was his personal discernment, not something among the truths that Jesus taught him. He taught clearly that *each has a particular gift from God, one having one kind and another a different kind.*[132] The call to live this or that way is not "fate." We believe that we are free to *lead the life that the Lord has assigned, to which God called you* personally and individually (1 Cor. 7:17). When we talk about "doing God's will" in our vocation, we refer to growing into the person God has hoped would realize his dream. But God has chosen his part: to hope, to patiently wait as we choose.

And that is the last thing to say about discerning a vocation. We believe that God is creating each person with gifts and talents oriented toward specific purposes and a way of life. God gave the Belgian Georges Lemaître a call to priesthood and also great mathematical abilities. He lived both by teaching as a priest at a Catholic university and as a mathematician proving for the first time that the cosmos had a beginning. (He was first to do this; in 1927 Albert Einstein only reluctantly and tardily admitted that Lemaître was correct.)

God our Creator invites us to a way of life by giving us gifts: all our talents, tastes, and skills, and even all our desires and aspirations. We have learned that every Christian (in fact, every human person) has a vocation. So what Bishop Jorge Bergoglio told his future priests about their vocation is also true of every one of us about ours: all of us "need to exercise the discerning generosity required for greater service in this specific mission,"[133] which is to be ourselves in our lifeworld.

This brings us to a final simplicity. The Holy Spirit is always leading us into God's dream. As the *Catechism* says at its end: "Love is the fundamental and innate vocation of every human being."[134] We act like fools when we forget that.

Touchstones

- The *sensus fidei* given by the Holy Spirit enables us to discern God's action in our nation's life narrative and in its present.
- Catholics must not fail to acknowledge that the Spirit is sowing grace in a huge range of social, medical, and educational services to the poor, sick, and needy.
- Acknowledging this work of the Spirit in our nation lays the foundation of gratitude under our discernment.
- God chooses our parents and our lifeworld, and our grace is to say yes to God's work in ourselves.
- The Spirit draws us into prayer, and each of us prays in a unique way. The prayer of consideration weaves Word and world together as we bring to God the concerns and events of ordinary life.
- We know God is infinite mercy; the spiritually mature also know that God is just, and we accept the gift of true fear of the Lord.

- The first discernment of vocation is that we are all called to live in Christ and to be his Mystical Body on earth. This is how we are a mission, in ourselves.
- Our personal vocations emerge in the gifts and desires with which God endows us. In and through our personal vocation, we are completing God's project on earth, his dream for each and all of us.

Practical Discernment

Practical discernment calls not only on mind and will but also on our whole self. Imagine Yo Yo Ma, the great American cellist, drawing his bow across his cello. The strings vibrate, but the sound comes not just from them but from the entire deep-chested instrument. That's how a disciple discerns. Not just the mind and not just prayer, but the whole deep self.

Yo Yo Ma is a masterful cellist. But an amateur can make the cello's rich sound, too, and even a beginner. The same is true of discernment. Some of us are gifted, some very practiced, and some just getting into it.

Ignatius of Loyola lived as a beggar and spent seven hours a day in prayer when he began his interior life. And he never let up. Almost in consequence, he was a master of discernment and codified the modern "discernment of spirits."

His disciple Jorge Mario Bergoglio prayed and studied for hours in the morning and another hour in the evening when he could control his own time. He learned to master his emotions and his desiring. Now as pope, he feels confident that he hears the Holy Spirit calling for reform of the Roman Curia and the decentralization of the Church.

PART SIX

GREAT HUMAN MYSTERIES

27

Jesus and the Grace of Failure

Christ's surrender calls for us to give our lives, and our lives are given by following the way of the Lord marked out on the cross.
—Pope Francis

We kneel before a crucifix and recall that death, a consequence of sin, has no power over Jesus of Nazareth. He hangs on a cross embracing death. At the end, *crying out in a loud voice*, Jesus deliberately *yielded up his spirit* (Matt. 27:50, NJB).

What can we believe about this faith handed on to us, so utterly contradictory to the human instincts and our sophisticated culture? We can believe that we contemplate a love so entire that the Son would want to embrace everything human—even suffering and death. We know what the faith teaches us: Jesus "sacrificed his life" for love of us. We struggle, though, to believe in a love so entire that it remains faithful when not returned. Unreturned love is a profound form of suffering. And Jesus' unreturned love was not just not returned; it was violently, disdainfully rejected.

No one will understand so great a love who has not experienced it. God knows that is true. He knew it about his own people. So God sent the Son to show us that love, and Jesus did so, publicly suffering rejection and execution.

As human love did for Jesus of Nazareth, our sin-pocked love will make us taste failure.

Then he invited us to *love one another as I have loved you* (John 15:12). If we do that, we will experience failure. For our love, "following the way of the Lord marked out on the cross," is weakened by selfishness and sin.[135] It will entail for us a whole range not only of joys but also of griefs and sorrows. As human love did for Jesus of Nazareth, our sin-pocked love will make us taste failure.

Jesus failed. We will fail. Some statistics reveal that about half of the Catholics married now were divorced earlier. Other people will fail us. Others failed Jesus. Look at the crucifix again: you are looking at utter, absolute human failure.

• • •

This is a deep mystery and a little frightening. Love that is all-powerful chooses to reveal itself humbly, not mightily, and not exacting a return of love, but humbly yearning for it. The leaders of the people were waiting to hear the *loud voice in heaven* that Daniel had promised, *proclaiming, "Now have come the salvation and the power and the kingdom of our God and the authority of his Messiah"* (Rev. 12:10). They did not hear that in Jesus. They waited for a powerful king, and this poor carpenter came riding on a donkey. He fulfilled some of the prophecies but contradicted the ones about triumph and power. But *Scripture must be fulfilled* (Luke 22:37). So from their point of view, the leaders discerned that *it is better to have one man die for the people than to have the whole nation destroyed* (John 11:50).

Jesus had failed them—as they understood Scripture—and they turned on him ferociously. They were his enemies, but his friends did little better. They all abandoned him. One of those closest to him betrayed him. Judas had taken a bag of money and despaired when that pittance was all his loyalty was worth. Then he made the fatal mistake of acting as his own judge—merciless, as God is not.

Another of Jesus' disciples tried to be brave and stay with him throughout his trial. He couldn't manage it and failed. Three times: *I do not know the man* (Matt. 26:74). Jesus had told Peter he would do this. But the Rock wanted to be near him. He risked it and lost. Some of us want to try this nearness, and some of us have risked it and lost. Maybe some marriages I have performed were like that; maybe some of the Jesuit priests who left and married were like that. All of us, when we mature, will know to be not like Judas, who destroyed himself, but like Peter, who knew bitter repentance.

Two other disciples fled Jerusalem. "They are leaving behind," Pope Francis says, "the 'nakedness' of God."[136] The nakedness of God? Yes: he's naked on the cross, and his love is naked, too. Love is not in every second beautiful, serene, fulfilled. So the ones from Emmaus failed him, too.

We fail, all of us, and sometimes we feel as naked as Jesus felt. I was once crushed by a fiercely negative evaluation, and I was naked in failure. Parents feel helpless when confronted by faithless offspring. A spouse sees nothing but misery in remaining faithful and staying. The alcoholic, sex addict, and drug user see themselves enslaved—bitter, bitter failures.

When we fail so far, we can follow Judas by focusing on our failure, and through that, end up focusing on ourselves. We can embrace our failure rather than God's mercy. This course is immature and leads to disaster. The mature disciple can discern the core of pride in this refusal to repent. It is satanic, literally. If we humble ourselves and let failure shape us, we can hand ourselves over to the Lord, just one more of his typical disciples. We can follow Peter, who at the end knew just this one thing: *Yes, Lord; you know that I love you* (John 21:15).

Peter was beginning to love the way Jesus loves, with this great difference: Jesus had not chosen his failure as Peter had. On the contrary, he urgently begged the Father to *remove this cup from me* (Luke 22:42). Jesus did not want to be put to death. When we face failure, the mature know to imitate Jesus and ask the Father to keep us from it, or it from us. *Beg* the Father. When God lets us fail, the mature know where the focus needs to be—and not be.

When failure blindsides us, if we reflect on this spiritually, we will likely wonder whether we brought it on ourselves. Did Jesus wonder about bringing this on himself? The thought may have lingered in Jesus' mind as he prayed. But he rejected it, insisting that *I have come down from heaven, not to do my own will, but the will of him who sent me* (John 6:38). Jesus went to his cross convinced that the Father wanted this to happen.

From this we can conclude that failure is a gift. It is a grace. God gives failure just as God gives success. Many fail and can see nothing but themselves failing, as Judas did. But the mature disciple can take failure as a mysterious encounter with the God who suffers as his love is not returned.

The *gift* of failure God gives to his chosen, who know how to find Jesus in it. This is a mysterious thing, but mature discernment yields a consoling conviction: when we fail, we join Jesus of Nazareth who failed. Perhaps weeping, we can say: *I will boast all the more gladly of my weaknesses, so that the power of Christ may dwell in me* (2 Cor. 12:9).

28

Discerning, Not Denying, Death

[T]hrough the working of the Spirit, there already exists in individuals and peoples an expectation, even if an unconscious one, of knowing the truth about God, about man, and about how we are to be set free from sin and death.

—Pope Francis

We buried my younger brother, Charles, in 1976. He was only forty-three and left his wife and six children. I drove their station wagon home after the burial. I sat in a rocker as my sister-in-law went into the kitchen to start life again. Their four-year-old son, Michael, climbed into my lap after the funeral. He buried his face in my shoulder, and his little voice said, "I want him back." I couldn't breathe for a minute. I just rocked a little and held him close.

As a little boy like Michael, Jesus of Nazareth had to learn about death and how his people grappled with it. All through human history, cultures have accepted this appalling finality in distinctive ways. Our secular culture has invented a new way: we deny it.[137] We do not claim that we won't die. Rather, we simply do not include death in our thinking about life. We brush it aside when we think about the meaning of human life. Brush aside? Most Americans go further, as one atheist wrote: people "deny it, repress it, dilute it, or otherwise hide it."[138] They do this to escape what he called the "death terror."

Christians, "knowing the truth about God, about man, and about how we are to be set free from sin and death," need not feel this terror.[139] Yet we are paying as little attention to death as do unbelievers. Many Catholics now omit the traditional wake and simply disappear the body. Clergy have abandoned the practice of urging us to prepare for a holy death. Homiletic materials hardly mention dying. A generation ago, Christians were eager to make sure we died a holy death. Catholics prayed earnestly for our dead, that they have been taken into God. We don't do much of either anymore.

Mature disciples face death confidently and fold it into their discernment, as did Mother Teresa and many saints who left their thoughts in writing. Our faith is perfectly clear, and we know that we are already living the life of persons who are destined to eternal joy. St. Paul explained for the Jewish and pagan Christians in Rome that *we have been buried with him by baptism into death, so that, just as Christ was raised from the dead by the glory of the Father, so we too might walk in newness of life* (Rom. 6:4). His declaration is as startling to us as it was to them.

This *newness of life* removes all terror of death from the discerning heart. But we do well to go against current unmindfulness and keep ourselves mindful of death. We can detail three ways a good Christian can appreciate death, each more mature than the former:

Our faith is perfectly clear, and we know that we are already living the life of persons who are destined to eternal joy.

- Death is an ordinary event in earthly life.
- Death inflicts the severest of the punishments for sin.
- Death integrates into full Christlife those the Father has chosen.

First, we can consider death an ordinary event in human life. As the agnostic Steve Jobs felt, "Death is the destination we all share," and that's that.[140] But he took a noble approach, calling death "the single best invention of life," because it clears away old life for the new. Perhaps this noble mindset prepared Jobs to die well, for his dying words were, "Oh wow! Oh wow! Oh wow!" He said this three separate times, looking directly at something or someone beyond those in the room, a something that thrilled him with delight. Not even his wife can tell what he saw or what "wow" meant; we can hope and pray that he now knows the whole truth.[141]

Christians, however, do not acquiesce in death merely as "the destination we all share," as Jobs did. It's not a final destination at all. It's a door. If it feels a bit final to us, that's because the death of a body with an immortal soul is not "natural" but is the effect of sin.

This raises the second way of appreciating death: as the punishment of sin. The earliest humans were not to die. So as the *Catechism* puts it, death is one of the worst of the "tragic consequences of this first disobedience."[142] Death makes its entrance into human history after the story had begun.

Christians can face death with respect rather than with the blankness or terror of those who think that a human life simply ends—*kaput*, nothing. Our faith teaches us that we go on living forever. Our faithful hearts sense that the choice of *how* we will go on living must be safeguarded by our present discernment and how we act because of it. The mature disciple discerns this without fear: we die the way we have lived. And we can expect to continue on that same trajectory for a long, long while.

That "long while" raises an alternative: hell. It is true that Christians do not now cringe at the thought of a fiery hell. Yet we cannot deny that somehow, somewhere, those who have deliberately, over long periods of life, denied God and Christ and done hideous evil to neighbor—are going to wish they had lived differently. I wonder whether anyone would want to share the eternal trajectory of the defeated Nazi leader who poisoned his six children, his wife, and then himself. I am quite sure that I do not.

Occasionally, the wise of the world claim to have evidence that our belief in an afterlife is just a way of escaping the death terror. The mature (the "little ones" to whom the Father reveals truth) know better. Belief in an afterlife, it has to be noted, gives us the grace of fear of the Lord and makes us soberly consider how we are living. How we are living, actually, is *in union with Christ Jesus*, which imposes responsibilities on us (Rom. 8:1).

This brings us to the third way of appreciating death. Christians who are spiritually mature anticipate dying in union with Jesus Christ. We have lived in union with him, and this gives us courage. We are sinners, it is true, but we are given the consoling belief that we will not be condemned for our sins. For the law of the Spirit, which brings us union with Christ Jesus, has set us free from the law of sin-and-death (see Rom. 8:2).

Well, then, we correctly pray for a peaceful death. Some may be invited to endure a long illness, though we are no longer likely to suffer intolerably. We do well to stay mindful, however, that for a full century now, Christians are joining Christ in heroic martyrdom.[143] Archbishop Oscar Romero and the Jesuit martyrs of San Salvador stand out, but they stand in a huge cohort of martyrs, some as heroic as they were and some anonymous and hidden.

We have all heard of St. Maximilian Kolbe and St. Edith Stein, who were murdered by the Nazis. And most have seen the photograph of Fr. Miguel Pro being shot to death while proclaiming "Viva Cristo Rey!" But the murder of Christians for living and proclaiming our faith marks the whole twentieth century. Many were individuals: Sr. Dorothy Stang was shot in the Brazilian jungle while proclaiming the gospel. Many were communities: in Rwanda, some 200 sisters, clergy, and laymen were martyred because they preached the gospel and denounced the genocide. We can still watch on the Web the beheading of twenty-one Coptic Christians by Islamic fanatics because they persisted in their "unbelief." The numbers are huge and appalling—such that popes and scholars call the past century the bloodiest in Christian history. During the civil war in Spain, for instance, anti-Christians killed 7,000 Catholics. Their names were sent to the Vatican, but 300,000 Christians in North Korea have vanished, nameless and without a trace. This martyrdom continues in the Middle East and in Africa and truly all around the world, some few publicized but most quite hidden.[144]

Among the hidden was a little Mexican boy. José Sanchez del Río was not yet fifteen in 1928 when he insisted on riding with the Cristero army in Mexico to fight against the insanely anti-Catholic Plutarco Elías Calles. The boy was captured and tortured. He wept and screamed when slashed with machetes, but he kept shouting, "Viva Cristo Rey!" The soldiers promised to spare his life if he denied Christ. When he would not, they bayonetted him and finally shot him. As he was dying, he drew a cross in the dust and kissed it, "knowing the truth about God, about man, and about how we are to be set free from sin and death."[145]

29

Enacting Good News That Still Surprises

The Gospel tells us that when the first disciples went forth to preach, "the Lord worked with them and confirmed the message" (Mark 16:20).
The same thing happens today.
—Pope Francis

Imagine your response if good Pope John XXIII were to tap on your door and stick his head in to chat. You would find it hard to believe, even if he lit a cigarette. The current pontiff might show up in person, considering the way Pope Francis does things. But a visitor from the past—pope, president, or great-grandmother? We'd be incredulous.

This is certainly how Jesus' disciples felt about his rising from the dead: incredulous. Actually, it was worse than that: they were *startled and terrified, and thought that they were seeing a ghost* (Luke 24:37). No one believed the silly stories about the dead coming back. Frankly, it's still hard to believe. I cannot easily imagine St. John Berchmans showing up in the sickroom of a dying little nun back toward the swamps in Grand Coteau.[146]

The faith proclaimed to us, however, is crystal clear: we will live forever as we are now, enfleshed spirits, minus aches and pains, doubts and fears. The Holy Spirit empowers us to believe and hope for what is beyond human ability to achieve. Yet more than one opinion poll gives discouraging news about what Christians say about life after death. That goes a considerable distance toward explaining why we seem to live like everyone else.

Even mature disciples have trouble really hearing that we will live in our flesh forever. For the Church has not spent much time and energy witnessing to the resurrection and eternal life of the body. Theologians haven't studied it, either, as Karl Rahner said in the very last address he gave.

A story told in the Gospel of Mark offers ambiguous help. The Sadducees did not accept *that there is a resurrection* and tested Jesus' belief with a well-worn case. *Now there were seven brothers; the first married a wife and then died leaving no children.* Then the second married her and died, then the third, and so on down through the seventh. *Now at the resurrection, when they rise again, whose wife will she be, since she had been married to all seven?* (Mark 12:18–23, NJB).

Jesus' response to the Sadducees challenges us as it challenged them. First, Jesus said that *when they rise from the dead* they do not marry, but *they are like the angels in heaven* (Mark 12:25). It's easy to get this wrong. I have heard plenty of devout Catholics say they believe they will rise in a *spiritual* body, like angels—as though Jesus' wounds were not physical and his eating breakfast with the disciples were a pretense.

But Jesus did not say that we will be like angels because we won't have bodies. We will be like angels because our holiness and integrity will be crystal clear. After rising, men and women may not marry, but if we go to heaven already married, we can expect that to stick. Anyhow, in my family, if Mercedes Mullen and Joe Tetlow Sr. got to heaven and were told they had to split, I'm pretty sure they would have packed up and moved Somewhere Else. (That's not revealed theology, but believe me, they at least would have tried it. Having raised children in New Orleans, they know a lot about heat.)

We will be like angels because our holiness and integrity will be crystal clear.

Anyhow, about the seven brothers for one bride, we have to say we don't know how the Father will untangle that one. Not to worry: *as for the dead rising again*, Jesus turns to Moses *in the passage about the bush* (Mark 12:26, NJB). He reminds the Sadducees (and us) that God told Moses, *I am the God of Abraham, the God of Isaac and the God of Jacob.* That might mean that God was alive when Abraham lived and God was still alive when Isaac lived and then Jacob, too. But that's not what Jesus means.

Jesus means that the patriarchs are alive right now. *He is God, not of the dead, but of the living* (Mark 12:27, NJB). That trio are still alive. When each of them died, he escaped the limit of time. Through that door, they started to live *now*, no yesterday and no tomorrow, just *now*. For God is not limited by time; in God everything is *now*. Abraham and Isaac and Jacob are still alive, not bare souls without flesh; they are not like angels in an airy existence. They are alive as themselves, enfleshed spirits, enspirited flesh—head, heart, and hands. For "after death the righteous will live for ever with the risen Christ," and they will come with Jesus and all the angels and other saints for the *Parousia*, the Last Judgment.[147]

There is a lot we do not know about that Last Judgment and life after death. The Church now teaches that God has revealed the resurrection of the body only gradually, step by step.[148] In my experience, God has not completed the revelation. The *Catechism* admits what troubles everyone's mind: "But how can we believe that this body, so clearly mortal, could rise to everlasting life?"[149]

The response has to be that living this truth is a supernatural gift from God. None of us knows how we are so sure of this resurrection. I know only that I am sure. Jesus told us, *I am the resurrection*, and when I accepted him, I embraced the Resurrection. The *Catechism* says it: "Christ will raise us up 'on the last day'; but it is also true that, in a certain way, we have already risen with Christ."[150] As St. Paul told the Romans, *just as Christ was raised from the dead by the glory of the Father, so we too might walk in newness of life* (Rom. 6:4).

Well, maybe that's a little help. If I have already risen in Christ and walk on my own feet in newness of life, why would I exist only as a ghost after death, as the Greeks were sure they would? It is true that in that coming event of the *Parousia*, we *also will be revealed with him in glory* (Col. 3:4). But in that lapse between the time I go through my death and when the end-time comes for everyone on earth—God is always my God, still the God of the living, not of the dead.

So mature discernment yields a joyful thought: my end-time comes when my time here is done. Death is the "end-time" for me. As I wait for that, I live with a lively eagerness to have breakfast with Jesus on some shore. He will have made strong coffee, and when I ask for it really strong, everyone will know that it's me.

The mature discerner knows that Pope Francis is correct: "Christ's resurrection is not an event of the past; it contains a vital power which has permeated this world."[151] If we live as though we really believe that, the Lord will work with us "and [confirm] the message . . . the same thing [will happen] today" as happened all through the centuries: others will come to Christ.[152]

30

Discernment and the Mystery of Pain

[B]oth physical and spiritual pain are borne from within, where no one can enter; it entails a great deal of solitude.

—Cardinal Jorge Mario Bergoglio, Pope Francis

Suffering strikes us Americans as a problem to be solved. We have had good success solving the problems of physical pain. Happily, too, we are learning how to reduce psychological pain to manageable levels. Unhappily, we Americans have ways of dealing with spiritual pain: repress it or medicate it. We deny death and turn our eyes from the millions of suffering people in our time. We ask ourselves, despairingly, *Who can heal that vast problem?*

No one, actually. The reason is that suffering is not a problem to be solved. Suffering is a mystery to be lived. We will never be able to understand why God wills or even allows suffering. This is one of the hardest teachings of the faith to embrace without feeling like a wretch or a little weird. God does let us suffer, even as children.

We humbly admit that we do not understand this mystery. Discerning Christians do not try to defend this lack of understanding. We are bound by time, limited, and immersed in mysteries. But if we cannot *understand* suffering, our *discernment* can move deeper and deeper into the mystery of it in our hearts and actions.

St. Paul told the Colossians that Jesus had established the reign of God and reconciled them and made them holy. But those who are chosen as his sisters and brothers will suffer, as he did. St. Paul put it this way: *God chose to reveal his Son in me.*[153] For though we are living his risen life, we are living it in a suffering world. So the apostle Paul told friends, *It makes me happy to be suffering for you now, and in my own body to make up all the hardships that still have to be undergone by Christ for the sake of his body, the Church* (Col. 1:24, NJB). The mature disciple can discern in prayer that this is true of us, too.

St. Paul is not saying that Jesus did some of the suffering of humanity and then left the rest for us to finish. No. Jesus served the Father *by finishing the work that you gave me to do*, and his last words on the cross were *It is finished* (John 17:4; 19:30). But he also promised that those who follow him will take up their own cross daily. The sufferings St. Paul was glad to share were not the sufferings of Jesus of Nazareth. They were the sufferings of the Body of Christ in Paul's day. We take up our own cross when we go through the sufferings imposed on the Body of Christ by the sins of our own day.

As Jesus of Nazareth embraced suffering when he became flesh, each of us embraces suffering as we grow in the flesh. *Servants are not greater than their master* (John 15:20). Accepting this truth, we can fathom the truth that our own sufferings are redemptive—not for our own selves, merely, but for *his body, the Church*.

We take up our own cross when we go through the sufferings imposed on the Body of Christ by the sins of our own day.

A mother watches her son waste his life on drugs and aimless wandering. She can do nothing. She just suffers, watching her son. Is God indifferent to him and to her? No. God in Christ knows suffering, too. Christ loves that man-child to the point of dying for him and is heartbroken to watch the waste. That mother is filling up the afflictions that Christ has to undergo today. Our experience is that "spiritual and physical pain are borne from within, where no one can enter; it entails a great deal of solitude."[154]

However, my suffering is not just about me. Our belief is that we suffer for a purpose. We suffer as Jesus did: to save humankind from itself. He said to the Father: *As you have sent me into the world, so I have sent them into the world*, and Jesus was sent to share humanity's pain (John 17:18). So our suffering is one of the things we were sent into the world to do as we are taken into Christ's project to save humankind. We are invited to share his suffering. My response to this, one anguished retreat day, was the murmured prayer, "I am so honored."

• • •

Does this explain suffering? No. The meaning of suffering hides in its mystery. I never really grasped the theology explaining why suffering is necessary. I certainly do not understand why the innocent suffer. And most of all, why did Jesus of Nazareth, sinless and innocent, have to go through what he went through? I think it was St. Augustine who said that every child of God on earth suffers, but only One suffers guiltless. But how does that help?

I *want* to understand. I want to understand suffering so badly that I sometimes become angry at not understanding it. A communist artist in Rome once challenged Cardinal Bergoglio that Jesus must have felt angry at the injustice as he hung on the cross. "I never thought of it like that," the cardinal said, "but perhaps Christ, in his humanity, was in some way angered by his dreadful suffering."[155]

If he was angered, he had an experience many of us have. We are likely to become angry *at* suffering as though our suffering were an enemy. If it lasts a long time, we can grow angry with it, wanting it to "just go away! Why can't they do something about this?" But if Jesus was angry at his suffering, he did not show it. He just went through it.

We do not find it easy to just go through it. Whenever I suffer, I know that he who "just went through it" has been where I am. I am in the Body of Christ in a world viciously marred by sin. I am in communion in that Body. It is true that suffering is private and a deeply personal affair. But when I suffer, I enter the zone where Christ now dwells. I am in communion with all those who suffer. This is not myth any more than breast cancer or a prolapsed heart valve is myth.

For the person who is growing in his or her discernment, then, our suffering does not isolate us. We recognize that in suffering we are in deeper communion with humankind than we could be if we only felt sorry for those who suffer. This may be a mystical experience because only the "little ones"—the humbled—grasp it.

I found among my mother's papers a little square note she had posted above her desk after my father died. She wrote, "Peace floods my soul and what was a burden to carry alone, became a joy sharing it with Christ." Then she volunteered to teach little children in an Alaskan mission. She had discerned in her sorrow *the way and the truth* and lived patient and content, going to help the little people freezing on the margins.

Touchstones

- Jesus of Nazareth did not have to die. The Son chose to join us even in this, the dire sequel to our sins.
- As a worker and prophet, Jesus of Nazareth was a human failure.
- God gives the gift of failing to those he chooses.
- We want to handle our failures the way Peter handled his, not the way Judas did.
- Each of us faces death and can think of it in three ways: as fate, as punishment for sin, and as joining Jesus Christ in his project.
- Jesus' disciples were aghast at his risen presence, and we still have trouble imagining enfleshed eternal life—which is promised to us.
- Pragmatic Americans think of suffering as a problem to be solved. We disciples of Christ are taught better: suffering is a deep mystery to be lived.
- When we suffer, we are entering one of Jesus Christ's zones—the other one being promised to us when it's over.

A New Christian Humanism

Pope Francis opposes the fear or denial of death with the characteristics of a new Christian humanism. Refusing to give an abstract discourse on what he observes of it in the Church, he simply notes three qualities.

The first quality is *humility*, wanting to serve and help. "Obsession with preserving one's glory, one's 'dignity,' one's influence must not play a part in our sentiments."* We are all sinners saved.

The second is close to that: *disinterest*. We are not struggling for self-fulfillment or success. Instead, we are steadily watchful of the interests and happiness of people, creatures, or any part of creation God places in our lives. As the pope puts it, "Christian humanity always goes forth. It is not narcissistic or self-referential."

The third quality is *beatitude*: living the Beatitudes. Here is the contrary of human happiness, built on having plenty of pleasure, money, and health. Instead, we learn from the simplest, humblest people among us that this beatitude "is that of one who knows the treasure of solidarity, of sharing even the little that one possesses; the treasure of the daily sacrifice of a job, hard and poorly paid at times, but performed out of love for loved ones; and also that of one's poverty, which however, when lived with trust in the providence and mercy of God the Father, nourishes a great humility." Those who are truly poor and those of the affluent who go to help for a while can recall the joy of this experience.

In reality, Christian humanism is quite revolutionary—it always has been—because it is guided not by the spirit of the times—Renaissance, Enlightenment, Postmodernism—but by the Holy Spirit of the God who poured himself out for us. The discerning Christian recognizes this. We also recognize the challenge that *humility, disinterest, and beatitude* present to us.

*All the citations are from the Address to the Fifth Convention of the Church in Italy, November 10, 2015.

PART SEVEN

DEEPER PERSONAL MEANING

31

Discernment Enables Us to Worship the God of Gods

But since we all have need to worship—because we have the imprint of God within us—when we do not worship God, we worship creatures.
—Pope Francis

I was surprised that my elderly mother asked me to bless her state lottery ticket. "Ma—bless a *lottery ticket*?" Well, if she won the million dollars, she could give a hundred thousand to the diocese in Fairbanks where she'd volunteered to teach little children. Then she would give fifty thousand to the Jesuit missions. Then fifty thousand here and fifty thousand there—until she had given away more than she'd won. I blessed the ticket.

My mother knew that this little god, chance, does some real work. She didn't think of it as a god, as none of us do. But the faith teaches that God is the God of gods, and my mother's hope was that the One who is in charge of this little god would put it to work. Hence the blessing. To finish the tale, the ticket I blessed didn't win. So mother bought another one, every week until she died, with a Hail Mary. I didn't bless any of them. They still didn't win.

The first discernment starts in the revelation that God is the God of gods, *the Father, from whom are all things and for whom we exist* (1 Cor. 8:6). But if we look deeply into ourselves, we find in our hearts a feeling for other "gods," and the discerning person recognizes that we sometimes feel that there *are* other gods. Pope Francis gently pointed that out in a homily: "We all have within ourselves some hidden idol. We can ask ourselves, in the sight of God: what is my hidden idol? What takes the place of God?"[156]

Writing larger about the secularism of Western culture, Pope Francis also pointed out that we act as though there were little gods. "The worship of the ancient golden calf (cf. Ex 32:1–35) has returned in a new and ruthless guise in the idolatry of money and the dictatorship of an impersonal economy."[157] This is an appreciative awareness of how *the law of sin and death* operates in our secular everyday life (Rom. 8:2).

The faith handed on to us was first revealed when the exiled Israelites found little gods everywhere. Moses instructed the people as they journeyed: *Do not follow other gods, any of the gods of the people who are around you*, for *your God is the God of gods, the Lord of lords* (Deut. 6:14; 10:17). Those *other gods* teemed in the neighborhoods of the early Israelites: Baal was the showiest, but the Jebusites, Amorites, and Philistines all had their gods, too. In Jesus' lifetime, the Romans, by a casual count of a standard list, served about two hundred little gods: Obarator was the god of ploughing; Pax, goddess of peace; Janus, god of doors and beginnings; Fortuna, goddess of fate; Ceres, goddess of crops and fertility; and so on and on.

St. Paul warned the Philippians against those whose *minds are on earthly things* and whose *belly is their god* (see Phil. 3:19). (The apostle's text could be illustrated with today's ads for yard-wide pizza and half-pound, triple-layer hamburgers.) In a more tranquil mood, he told the Ephesians to look on a fornicator as *an idolater* sacrificing honor and health to a false god (Eph. 5:5). He was careful to remind the Corinthians that *we know that no idol in the world really exists, and that there is no God but one*, but then he had to add that *there are plenty of gods and plenty of lords* in the world (1 Cor. 8:4–5, NJB). They are always there to be served by the undiscerning.

Unless we complete the first great discernment, we will believe and enact faith in the little gods. Paul points out to the Galatians that *when you did not know God, you were enslaved to beings that by nature are not gods* (Gal. 4:8). Humans need something or someone greater than everyday reality "because we have the imprint of God within us." Consequently, "when we do not worship God, we worship creatures."[158] Every one of us might ask if we might not be pleasurably "enslaved" by what Pope Francis calls "unbridled consumerism."[159]

Unless we complete the first great discernment, we will believe and enact faith in the little gods.

• • •

That we are a sophisticated people does not mean we escape this sort of belief. The scientific mind recognizes the existence of mysterious natural forces. The most extensive of them is the "dark force," and recently, scientists have added "dark matter." A careful scientist might insist that these are natural, not supernatural—but they act a lot like gods who have pervasive, irresistible powers and total presence.

And right along with them, the less sophisticated all correctly list some other mysterious natural forces: chance, luck, destiny, beauty, wealth, fame, and a lot more. A businessman admitted to a group of us recently that the success of his latest venture had depended on pure chance. Even in this good Christian group, he did not mean it depended on God; he meant a god, dressed in a good business suit. "We have created new idols," Pope Francis wrote, even those of us who believe in Jesus Christ.[160]

Chance stands out among those little idols. Serious scientists believe that evolution comes about through strict Darwinian random selection. This is simply chance. They believe it embedded in the cosmos, current and in all past times. This chance transcends absolutely all events in time and space, and all events in time and space act according to this chance. That's a little god like some of the Greek godlings.

Coming closer to everyday experience, think of luck. Luck, many think, disposes real events. We wish good luck to our friends and pray for it (as my mother did). Luck is a palpable force, and luck is a false little god.

Success is a heavier deity in the secular pantheon. Success promises human fulfillment and happiness. It does not smile on everyone, and those whom it blesses are a radiant elite. One of the latter was a faithful Catholic man, call him Cody, whom I worked with in the Cursillo movement. When he finally faced his predicament, he said frankly that he had been worshipping "Success." Cody learned late. His marriage had been seriously damaged by his total dedication to success in his work. As his several children grew and settled down, they moved as far away from his home as they could. He and his wife never divorced, but they lived effectively, and often physically, separate.

It was a grace that he finally learned what it does indeed profit a man to gain total success and lose his self: nothing.

For that is the reward that the little gods give in the end: nothing.

The first task of discernment in this matter is to recognize that, indeed, we do serve these little gods and that our service can become a substitute religion. We ardently hope that Luck will bless us; we do penances for the sake of beauty; and we sacrifice far too much so we can reach the holy grail, Success. Each of these is serving one of the little gods. But serving them is so neatly woven into our everyday lives that we need to ponder and pray to appreciate how. We might also need to go back to reading about our forebears who won free of this substitute religion. Why not read about the saints whose lives can help us understand that "when we do not worship God, we worship creatures," as Pope Francis put it in the citation that begins this peculiarly difficult discernment? The saints' lives have a lot to tell us.

32

Discernment, through the Examen, Renews Our Minds

I think this is truly the most wonderful experience we can have: to belong to a people walking, journeying through history together with our Lord, who walks among us! We are not alone; we do not walk alone. We are part of the one flock of Christ that walks together.

—Pope Francis

Ignatius of Loyola elaborated the classic Examen for use in the thirty-day Spiritual Exercises. In his day, during the Renaissance and Reformation, people's self-appreciation was closely woven into their rank in society and their religious absolutes. As modernity dawned in the Western world, people's self-appreciation dissipated into individualism. Then we began to assess ourselves less by rank and any kind of absolutes and more by our psychological condition. We had let a distance, even a disconnect, grow between the real world around us and the inner world of our own selves.[161]

> We had let a distance, even a disconnect, grow between the real world around us and the inner world of our own selves.

Through this great change, many of us kept on doing the classic Ignatian Examen.[162] We did its five points: first, I thank God for the gifts he has given and is giving me right now. Second, I ask the grace of seeing my day and my life as the Holy Spirit sees them. Usually I am working on one particular characteristic or (also usually, bad) habit. Third, I review what I have actually enacted today. I say *enact* because I look at the gifts God is giving me and I ask how I have actually done with them. This is about action, but I do not ignore my feelings, desires, and intentions. After accusing myself before the Lord for any sins and acknowledging to myself where I have failed,

I move to the fifth moment. Parallel to the "purpose of amendment," I look at what tomorrow might bring and what I might do to better myself. As this new millennium dawned, even mature disciples unwittingly focused quite entirely on our individual selves in the Examen.

This classic exercise became hard to continue, even for me and my fellow Jesuits, though why was never very clear.[163] Perhaps it was because we had learned vastly more about the interweaving of conscience and the unconscious—about the brain, hormones, and human behavior—than had been available to St. Ignatius. Perhaps, also, because we were not clear how the Examen fed directly into discernment (we were more or less stuck on "discernment of spirits"). For whatever reason, some were able to continue the five-point Examen, but most of us tried other forms.

One other form of the Examen focused on the relationships in my life. It is meant to help keep them lively and holy and ordered to my relationship with Christ in God. Still another Examen focused on the graces I have been given, the gifts. It focused on one virtue at a time, such as faith or hope, or on one of the gifts of the Holy Spirit such as wisdom or counsel. The Gifts Examen, developing or deepening the virtues, came closer to dealing with head, heart, and hands.

In 1972, George Aschenbrenner introduced another form most of us know: the Examen of Consciousness. He described this as "a daily renewal and growth in our spiritual identity as unique flesh-spirit persons loved and called by God in the inner intimacy of our affective world."[164] This Examen has proven helpful, and a lot of people still use it. Though it focused on "the inner intimacy of our affective world," as we just read, those who used it grew aware of a "call which God causes to resound in the historical situation itself," as St. John Paul II put it. We were seeing the signs of the times in a new way: "In this situation, and also through it, God calls the believer."[165] At least among those who used the Consciousness Examen whom I listened to, this call involved principally the believer, not his or her lifeworld.

Nonetheless, the Consciousness Examen let mature disciples share in "truly the most wonderful experience we can have: to belong to a people walking, journeying through history together with our Lord, who walks among us."[166]

It moved the mature disciple into discernment by bringing us to greater self-awareness and appreciation for our graces and virtues. We learned to value what is in our hearts and what we do and what is in our heads. It helped keep our sins and limitations in sound perspective. This suited our individualism as the rigidity of modernity was fading into what serious thinkers (including Pope Francis) consider a new age. Now, spiritual writers focus the Consciousness Examen onto concrete events, persons, and affects.

A recent and instructive handbook on the Ignatian Examen moves that development along and demonstrates the change.[167] It recommends a series of exercises on peak experiences of people, events, emotions, or of the desires and values underlying them. Introducing his fresh approach, Mark Thibodeaux insists that the one making the Examen is exploring "with God *all* the facets" of life. "God and I look together with a *holistic* view of my life: my sins and my virtues, my failures and successes, the things I'm grateful for and the things that drive me crazy."[168] He recommends attention to the dynamic interaction among faith, believing, and enactment—head, heart, and hands.

Furthermore, he is writing as though he had heard the summons given by Pope Francis in his second encyclical: "The time has come to pay renewed attention to reality and the limits it imposes; this in turn is the condition for a more sound and fruitful development of individuals and society."[169] This concern for the environment will not happen until we have accepted conversion—intellectual, affective, and moral, and social-political as well—conversion from self-care to concern for the common good.

This will require a lot of self-examining. Sin as selfishness is never far from us. A sinful people, St. Paul warns, must *let the renewing of your minds transform you* (Rom. 12:2, NJB). The mature disciple sees the work of the Examen as the work of renewing our minds, transforming our hearts, and making sure we perceive and appreciate the indispensable grace of "the most wonderful experience we can have: 'to belong to a people walking, journeying through history together with our Lord, who walks among us! We are not alone; we do not walk alone.'"[170] We are with Christ in the messy communion of his people, struggling with the mess we have made of our earth.

33

Loving God: I Can Do That

Whenever we encounter another person in love, we learn something new about God.

—Pope Francis

Before I reached the age of five, I had four siblings. It must have been hard for me to feel adequate. My parents kept pushing me along with a new baby: a sister before I could walk, then a brother before I could talk, and then suddenly I was "the big one"—at four years and eight months.

In my earliest experience, I was lazy and an underachiever. I didn't study. I didn't promote myself as a singer. I was not the first one chosen for a team. It seems to me that I rarely organized anything or invited girls out.

However, by the time I was six or eight years old, I had been "the big one" for some years. So in my earliest experience, I instinctively moved to settle problems or conflicts. I remember once when I was in a movie theater, someone yelled, "Fire!" and I got up looking for what we had to do—what *we* had to do. It turned out to be a joke, but my instinct for leadership was not a joke. It was a characteristic that, at various times in my growing up, others found helpful, or enviable, or egotistical, or simply aggravating.

And since what you do is what you become, in my early life I led the way in the externals of holiness and became a victim of perfectionitis. The Dominican nuns who taught me—those splendid women who, barely out of the teenage years themselves, mothered hundreds and hundreds and mothered me—conveyed to me the glowing conviction that I was holy. They made me feel holy, and so I glowed. As a boy, I wanted keenly to be holy. At a Boy Scout Mass one time, I sang "Holy God We Praise Thy Name" so sweetly that the Scout Master told my parents he thought he was hearing an angel.

Yeah. Right. Then I met competition, sex, money, and failure. I found darkness, and I was not holy. Yet the holy yearning that the nuns' glowing love illuminated deep in my shadowy inner life grew and grew. The spiritual life seemed to me based on this: "Lord, you are so holy, we dare not say your Name. We are your people. We keep these thousand, thousand rules and liturgies to show that we are holy, though we are not, and You want us to be. So, *help*!"

But as God comes to us when we are baptized, so God waits to come to us when we are older. Grace comes not only once in baptism, but again and again throughout life. Some time ago, at the end of a day during which I kept busy proving that my negative self-image was quite accurate, I went to the chapel to recite Evening Prayer. After praying Psalm 72, reminding God the Father that the Son's reign on earth shall endure like the sun and the moon from age to age, I urged God my Creator and Lord to remember that Jesus Christ will save the oppressed (among whom I enrolled myself that evening) and he will rescue their lives; to him their blood is dear. Just then I was not feeling that my blood was dear, or anything else about me, either. This is what we mean by "desolation."

After the psalm came the little snippet of Scripture to ponder on. That Thursday evening it was from the first letter of Peter: *Since by your obedience to the truth you have purified yourselves so that you can experience the genuine love of brothers, love each other intensely from the heart* (1 Pet. 1:22, NJB). I caught my breath, and in an instant of utter honesty, I said out loud, "I can do that. I can do *that.* I can love like a brother, in sincerity." And I shed tears for a while.

> But as God comes to us when we are baptized, so God waits to come to us when we are older.

Like a lot of tears, these were a brew of bitter sorrow for my little love, and exultant happiness for the love I do know. I can do *that.* I can *love like a brother, in sincerity and in truth,* which is another translation of the verse. And I kept trying—never enough for the parents in my life, those who were my mothers and brothers and fathers and cousins—and never adequate to the little given me to do. But I kept trying, and I discerned a great truth that Pope Francis puts this way: "When we live out a spirituality of drawing nearer to others and seeking their welfare, our hearts are opened wide to the Lord's greatest and most beautiful gifts."[171]

I can in all candor tell myself that I have managed something, plainly led by the Holy Spirit. I had no notion of what I was really achieving as I pounded shards of philosophy and history into my brain, struggled to grasp what a dean or a spiritual director is supposed to be and do, and sat for hours trying to learn how to pray. But in the ambiguities and clarities of any given day, I can set myself to enact this love that is given in me. Just this one day I can listen with an open heart to what the first pope's first encyclical goes on to advise: *Rid yourselves, therefore, of all malice, and all guile, insincerity, envy, and all slander* (1 Pet. 2:1). I can probably get through today ridding myself of all of that, none of which I like in myself anyhow—or in anyone else, for that matter.

The mature disciple realizes that we are living love, day by day and in all directions. We learn to live around both our strengths and our weaknesses, like being born first or coming in last. We can expect to be tested by difficult issues: whether and when to practice birth control, whether to remarry after a spouse's death or after divorce has shown that a marriage was never the sacrament of matrimony. Many of the tertians (young Jesuit priests doing a final year of formation) I directed had their call to priesthood severely tested.

But in all of that, "Loving others is a spiritual force drawing us to union with God; indeed, one who does not love others *walks in the darkness* (1 Jn 2:11) *[remains] in death* (1 Jn 3:14), and *does not know God*" (1 Jn 4:8).[172] Pope Benedict XVI had already written that "love of neighbour is a path that leads to the encounter with God, and . . . closing our eyes to our neighbor also blinds us to God."[173] If I set myself to love and to be loved, I find the experience is not a path but a destination: "Whenever we encounter another person in love, we learn something new about God."[174] To encounter is opposed to contend against or to debate with. And we almost always learn something new about ourselves.

34

Discernment and Attachments

A certitude is not just advice, an intellectual conviction, or a saying. It is also a testament, an agreement among what you think, what you feel, and what you do.

—Pope Francis

We have to begin in our heads right now, asking what exactly we are certain of. What are our moral, social, and intellectual absolutes? However much the intelligentsia insist that all things are relative, in their minds, this statement *is* absolute: "Everything is relative." They can believe that because they imagine that "certitude" is only in the mind. We discern certitude pulsing among head, heart, and hands. We not only *know* certitudes, we *live* certitudes.

Interviewers once asked Archbishop Bergoglio about this. He summarized his penetrating answer with the statement cited above about "great existential certitudes made flesh."[175] His phrase is vivid: genuine certitudes do not reside merely in the mind; they penetrate the heart, and they are enacted in life. This is what he means by "certitudes made flesh." The person who lives them coherently bears witness to their truth and passes them on by enacting them, not by proselytizing or arguing.

Richard Dawkins is an atheist, and he has created his testament to atheism. Pope Francis put it this way: Dawkins has made "the method and aims of science and technology an epistemological paradigm which shapes the lives of individuals and the workings of society."[176] Thus, with "scientific method" he proves there is no God, which is not an issue electron microscopes and mathematical theories can handle. Dawkins has made his certitudes flesh in talk and print and gladly witnesses to his convictions.[177] He is absolute in believing that there is no intelligent design in the universe even as he has spent his entire life brilliantly uncovering intelligible design in all living things.

Dawkins actually believes with his whole heart that his mind is the ultimate source of truth; what he feels and does is not a part of it. His are "the great existential certitudes made flesh in the coherence of life" but in a profoundly erroneous way. This one thing is clear about him: he is deeply and tightly attached to his own way of thinking. He is so stuck in his materialist science that he cannot appreciate that Aristotle and Thomas Aquinas, Galileo and René Descartes, Karl Linnaeus and Louis and Madame Pasteur were also as thoroughly scientific as he is—and all believed in God. The doctor's attachment to his own mind's work limits his freedom.

We do well to note this because most of our passionate attachments come with very strong certitudes. We are *sure* that this is what we want; we are *convinced* that this is what we ought to do or to be. We need to be chary of this kind of absoluteness, mainly because God deals with us in the story of our lives, day by day. We need to remain flexible and open in mind and heart and not let absolute convictions or fixed ideas cloud our appreciation and trammel our freedom.

For the discerning disciple, certitudes begin in the word of God. Hence, the more discerning we hope to be, the more familiar we need to be with that word. We could almost say that we need an attachment to reading the Gospels and the apostolic letters. If our life situation allows it—permanent deacon, schoolteacher, retired people with good Catholic educations—we should be attached to spiritual reading that we can relish, but it has to start and continue in the Bible.

We need to remain flexible and open in mind and heart and not let absolute convictions or fixed ideas cloud our appreciation and trammel our freedom.

Study helps us grasp the force of attachments. Any attachment is like a string that attaches a pen to the clipboard on which you fill out a form. That string is going to limit and even determine where and how you fill in those forms. Again, an attachment is like a Velcro fastener: it sticks to itself but it sticks to everything else, too. An attachment connects many experiences beyond its primary object. If I am attached to the Latin Mass, I won't much embrace any of the new liturgy because it's all in English. We might think of an attachment as a magnet on a table covered with little metal filings: all of them will either be drawn to or repelled from it.

An attachment can be good. For instance, if those metal filings are our activities and God is the magnet, then the attraction is good. Or the Velcro attachment can stand for a habit of thinking well of good friends and also of everyone else. In a sense, all virtues are habits, an "existential certitude made flesh in a coherent life," to paraphrase a bit.

Most of the time, the word *attachment* implies this kind of stuck habit. We want to have a lot of them—the firm attachments to virtuous actions such as being kind and doing our work thoroughly. However, attachments are harmful when they become inordinate.

What are *inordinate* attachments? Or better, when is an attachment *inordinate*? The word itself suggests to the discerning person that such an attachment is out of order because it involves sin. At a retreat I learned of a wife and mother in a household where both she and her husband worked outside the home. She regularly came home from work and drank not one but two large glasses of wine. She was certain that she needed two. That might have been fine, not disordered at all. But the way this attachment lived itself out proved otherwise: she was uncooperative in the kitchen, cranky with the children, and argumentative with her spouse. Her spouse felt that his wife did fine with just one glass of wine in the evening. But that second nightly glass proved to be an attachment that bordered on gluttony and resulted in anger. Her attachment to it was disordered.

In the twenty-first century, in a culture of vast possibilities and incessant invitations to do new and good things, mature disciples appreciate the value of holy attachments. We *want* to be attached to attending Mass and to helping our neighborhoods flourish. We hope to be passionate about our career or work and to be sincerely attached to the people in it. We need to be deeply attached to our spouses, our parents, and our children. At the deepest level of our interior lives, we need to be personally attached to Jesus Christ.

This would be having "the great existential certitudes made flesh in the coherence of life"—head and heart and hands all moving in concert.[178] And from there, provided we are passionately indifferent to just about everything else, we can move forward in love of God.

Now we need to ponder what being passionately indifferent might mean.

35

Discernment Brings Us to Passionate Detachment

This virtue of the large and small is magnanimity. Thanks to magnanimity, we can always look at the horizon from the position where we are. That means being able to do the little things of every day with a big heart open to God and to others. That means being able to appreciate the small things inside large horizons, those of the kingdom of God.

—Pope Francis

"Passionate detachment" sounds to most of us like a contradiction in terms (call it an oxymoron, and it sounds even worse). This term needs a lot of unpacking.

A personal experience Pope Francis related helps us understand. A famous painting by Caravaggio, *The Calling of Saint Matthew*, hangs in San Luigi dei Francesi, a church in Rome, which Cardinal Jorge Bergoglio visited regularly when he was there. In the painting, Jesus stands near Levy's money table, pointing at him. Levy clutches his money bag to his chest, clearly astonished: *Me?*

What impresses the pope about the painting is Matthew's gesture of attachment to his money. He seems to be saying, "No, not me! I have money! My money!" His gesture shows how passionate he is about money. But the call is just the beginning of his story, because after the scene in the painting (whatever its reality was), Matthew leaves his money and follows after Jesus. He was attached, passionately attached—and he left it. This is what "passionate detachment" means.

After he was elected pope, Francis explained that he identifies with Matthew: he is a sinner called. The Jesuit pope did not say what he was passionately attached to. But he has shown in the coherence of his life what his passionate detachment had to include: leaving a web of great friends in Buenos Aires and giving up being a simple priest among the poor, as he had planned to be when he retired as archbishop. And Francis's radiant joy shows how the Holy Spirit cherishes the "virtue of the large and small . . . magnanimity."[179]

What about us? We are most evidently attached to things. Americans are passionate about the *new*—car, clothes, iPads. We think, feel, and act as if we must have the newest things we can afford. (Why does advertising work?) This passion for the new becomes an "existential certitude made flesh in the coherence of life." But it's not a good way of life because "the accumulation of constant novelties exalts a superficiality which pulls us in one direction."[180] That direction is away from discernment that keeps us living the central truths and beliefs brought us by Christ. "It becomes difficult to pause and recover depth in life." That's the trouble with disordered attachments. This is what Francis condemns as "extreme consumerism" and "compulsive consumerism."[181]

But we may also have to give up attachments that are perfectly orderly in themselves. We may have to be passionately detached from really good things. A widow coming to retirement was deeply attached to the home her children grew up in. But her children kept worrying about her, and she generously chose to give up her beloved place and move. Two business-school graduates I knew were attached to their cars when they got engaged. But they knew they would have to make do with one when they married. So they got started on it. The decision that no blessed thing will stand between us and our love for God and for those whom God gives us to love signals a passionate detachment.

Most of the time, our attachments are good and holy enough. Think of activities you really enjoy, that are habitual, that you are really attached to—say, Saturday coffee with friends, watching pro ball with your grown sons, or regular aerobic exercise in a gym. Now imagine a situation in which you see clearly that you will have to choose between doing what you love and caring for an elderly parent. Which do you choose? If you remain as passionate about your attachment but go and do what love and honor of parents requires—then you are passionately detached.

You love golf. It's Sunday, and you choose either Mass with the family or golf with friends. Which is it? You do not despise either golf or your love for it when you choose Mass. Or, you love Scotch, a lot. You are put on some antibiotics that interact badly with alcohol. Now the choice is either dealing prudently with your physical self or enjoying the Scotch you love. You won't love the Scotch any less as you refrain from it for a while. But if you drink water for the time being, you'll be loving yourself (and God) more.

Spiritual detachment requires accepting my true feelings and ideas but wanting to follow them only insofar as they lead me toward God. The more we are aware of the things and people and experiences that we are passionate about, the better we can discern where the Holy Spirit is inviting us in the welter of our affections and the tangle of our minds. For one thing, the Holy Spirit often inspires in us a passionate desire for what God wants done next. That certainly seems to be happening in Rome these days.

> Spiritual detachment requires accepting my true feelings and ideas but wanting to follow them only insofar as they lead me toward God.

At times, the matter is serious. This really happened: you are well married and have children in their early twenties. You find yourself falling in love with a colleague. You know the deep gratification of being truly in love—you have been for years, though the early excitement of it has faded with diapers, teenagers, work routine, and simple tedium. So you have a choice. It's great to be in love. So do you maintain a passionate detachment toward this wonderful human experience coming along in a new love—or do you decide to follow the passion and attach your life to a new star that twinkles with a light other than Christ's?

That is detachment—passionate detachment. Maintain this attitude, and you'll live at peace in Christ. Without it, you are going to make some mistaken decisions. With it, you will have the greathearted outlook that impresses Pope Francis:

> This virtue of the large and small is magnanimity. Thanks to magnanimity, we can always look at the horizon from the position where we are. That

means being able to do the little things of every day with a big heart open to God and to others. That means being able to appreciate the small things inside large horizons, those of the kingdom of God.[182]

Touchstones

- We consider that worship of "the God of gods" suggests that there are still other little gods around.
- If we look into our hearts, we find that we serve some things or causes as though they were god: luck, beauty, money, an ideology or theory.
- Success is one of the little gods that cause us a lot of grief.
- The Ignatian Examen has a classical form (five points) and remains helpful in our postmodern time.
- When we are younger, we are more influenced by our rearing; maturity brings us to reach out and find others to love.
- An attachment (some of them passionate) is a habit of mind or heart or hands that can help us live virtuously or bring us into temptation.
- Passionate detachment means putting God first and being able to do the little things and look to the great things with magnanimity.

Some Odd Heresies

Pope Francis has been quite scathing in his denunciation of the new worship of the golden calf. As he sees it, yielding total control to "the market" and refusing to enable civil authorities to seek out and solve the resulting moral issues and social sin—this is "worshipping the golden calf."

But others are noting other, old heresies. Nathan Stone, for instance, an American Jesuit laboring among the people of the Amazon, recently named in his blog traces of Pelagianism.

This is the first of the two that Pope Francis noted just as I was writing this. He sees Pelagianism in some peoples' rigidly defining Christian life in terms of one cause or doctrine—liturgy, abortion, authenticity. "Christian doctrine is not a closed system, incapable of raising questions, doubts, inquiries, but is living, is able to unsettle, is able to enliven."*

The other ancient error Pope Francis noted is gnosticism. He had already thrown light on it in *The Joy of the Gospel*, rejecting "a purely subjective faith whose only interest is a certain experience or a set of ideas and bits of information which are meant to console and enlighten, but which ultimately keep one imprisoned in his or her own thoughts and feelings."

Strong language from a pope. He has been emphatic about reforming the Roman offices and decentralizing authority to where, in our ancient tradition, it belongs. He sees that those who are "concerned with being at the centre" always end "caught up in a web of obsessions and procedures."

This is not only Rome, and not only Washington, D.C. Each of us has to watch that we are not putting ourselves at the center and, failing in discernment, becoming obsessed with rules and procedures, causes and devotions. Christian humanism always reaches out, not narcissistic, not self-preoccupied, any more than our Master Jesus Christ was.

*Other than the one noted, all citations are from the Address to the Fifth Convention of the Church in Italy, November 10, 2015.

PART EIGHT
DISCERNMENT AND SIN

36

Encountering Christ in a Sinful World

[O]n the cross . . . Jesus endured in his own flesh the dramatic encounter of the sin of the world and God's mercy.

—Pope Francis

We need to understand the "sin of the world," or we are not likely to feel the real joy of knowing God's mercy. Start with a metaphor. Flannery O'Connor died of lupus erythematosus. Lupus is inherited: her father had it in the genes he inherited, and he passed it on to her in the genes she inherited. So a disease that was in her lifeworld was also in her from the day she was born. As she matured, so did those genes. She died at age thirty-nine of her ancestors', her father's, and her own genetic lupus erythematosus.

The genes in her family, her parents' genes, and then her own: that's how sin works in the world. Sin is spread through humankind, almost as an inheritance. Real sins are bred in and bestowed on me by my family and teachers. I take the sins in, then I enact them, confirming them and leading to my need to be saved "from this body of sin" that St. Paul grieved about. The work of sin is not past history: it is our story today.[183]

An unremitting force, sin seeps into everything human, even into human inventions meant to do nothing but good. The democracies that emerged in the past century were meant to bring freedom and plenty to their people but instead have brought "the widespread and deeply rooted corruption found in many countries—in their governments, businesses and institutions."[184] Our own economy has produced tremendous good, but not only good. "Today's economic mechanisms promote inordinate consumption," an evil in itself.[185]

These same mechanisms produce great wealth—for the very, very few. And "unbridled consumerism combined with inequality proves doubly damaging to the social fabric."[186] We meant the economy to spread the wealth; instead, it has concentrated it in the treasuries of a very few, deprived the great majority, and our nation is now divided, tense, and explosively violent with regular killings reaching the extreme of the mass murder of 49 people in Orlando, Florida, in June 2016.

An unremitting force, sin seeps into everything human, even into human inventions meant to do nothing but good.

This is sin-in-the-world. No amount of "progress" will obliterate it. But that does not make us despair. As powerful as sin is, it will not destroy the universe. Rather, we are told that from the beginning until now the entire creation has been groaning in one great act of giving birth (Rom. 8:22). Its power, though, is appalling: remember Auschwitz, Pol Pot, Gaza, 9/11, and ISIS. Watch the news tonight. We see this sin in vivid color, even if we rarely call it sin in all the violence.

• • •

Now turn to sin-in-me. We understand that sin-in-the-world becomes sin-in-me, though we find it hard to grasp how sin can survive the supernatural grace of baptism. Theologians have wrestled with that issue. The scholastic thinkers settled on the *relicta peccati*, the leftovers of sin: a weakening of the will to do good and to avoid evil. We can take a cool shower after too long on a beach, but our damaged skin burns on—*relicta peccati*, the leftovers from sin.

Perhaps with our clearer understanding of the unconscious, early conditioning, and addiction, we can well understand that the world's sin comes into our mind, our heart, and our hands. Think of it: the offspring of lying people will be given to lying—that's how they come to communicate. Children of racially prejudiced parents will be convinced racists—the parents' sin in their young's racial slurs. The son of alcoholic parents is liable to alcoholism—brain structure plus environment.

Daughters who are despised by their mothers will struggle not to despise their daughters. Sons of violent fathers will become violent fathers themselves unless they struggle to behave otherwise. I helped a couple prepare for marriage; he had been beaten by his father. Not a year into their marriage, they showed up at my door very late one night. She had an ugly black eye, and they were both scared, holding hands. I hugged them both, and we began to lay to rest the ghost of the violent father.

St. Paul's understanding of how all this fits together gives us the revealed truth that we have to live with: *Every time I do what I do not want to, then it is not myself acting, but the sin that lives in me* (Rom. 7:20, NJB). This is good news—that sin lives in me? Descendants of Rousseau and the Enlightenment, we want to hold our souls in newborn innocence. We can't, because they're not.

The mature disciple will hold on to this truth: every one of us will enter into discernment with this weight on his or her spirit. Even as we yearn to find what God wants for us—and work through our genetic inheritance, our rearing, and the forces of the world to which we are linked—we keep falling into our besetting sins. The bottom line: I commit sins.

The alcoholic chooses to drink, then to drink and drink—precisely the point of sin-in-me, but where's the line at my-sin? We feel more clearly the sins and shame of our society than we feel our own sins and shame—that's a characteristic of our culture. Society's sins are blared all over newspapers and television: Ferguson, children abused in their homes, homelessness, lying officials, violent police and demonstrators.

Sometimes, though we are quite clear that we have incurred guilt, we struggle to make a clean separation between the experience of this sin-in-me, which is not my fault, and my personal sin, which is. Where am I just a flawed, broken human being, and where am I deliberately sinning? When have rearing and trauma taken my freedom, and where ought I maturely reclaim it? The apostle who pointed this out knew no solution. He flung himself on God's mercy, *who will rescue me from this body of death? Thanks be to God through Jesus Christ our Lord* (Rom. 7:24–25).

He was not alone. None of us has a solution; we all need God's mercy because we all sin. We sin as much as St. Paul did, so we live a penitent life. In my act of contrition, I always ask Jesus Christ to "help me bear the burdens that sin has laid on me." As Karl Rahner said, we're in purgatory. We're being purged of sin and sinfulness.

The discerning disciple will recognize that we can claim the experience that Jesus had on the cross: "the dramatic encounter of the sin of the world and God's mercy."[187] Of course, sin-in-the-world struck him in an unjust condemnation and brutal execution. It strikes me when I make my own the sins that I inherited. Still, Jesus knows this encounter: our sin and God's mercy. He knows it. He chose to know it so he could draw me after him into the Father's love and mercy.

37

My Sin and My Discernment

The Eucharist, although it is the fullness of sacramental life, is not a prize for the perfect but a powerful medicine and nourishment for the weak.

—Pope Francis

Each conversion of my heart has to begin either in my head or in my hands. I have to see what I am doing as contrary to God's mind and heart. Or I have to go through some experience that brings home to me that something I am about to do contradicts my faith and my beliefs.

There's much more to conversion of heart, of course. One question spiritual writers used to ask: How can a creature as little as I am do anything that would bother God? We have to face this question, because the mindset behind it places God far above us or far beyond us. We have learned to discern that God is most intimately with me and in me, working all the works I do as the Creator of all things. With that in mind, and remembering that *God is love* and wants my love, I can begin to grasp how my sin could hurt the heart of God (1 John 4:8).

Sin is first of all neglecting God's love. It may be worse, as I may be deliberately deciding to turn away and reject him. But in either case, I am turning a cold heart to the One who has loved me before anyone else did. "God asks for shelter in the warmest part of ourselves: our heart," Pope Francis told the bishops of Brazil.[188] If I give him instead a cold heart, I am guilty of hurting his love.

> Anyone who does a grave sin is drawing God into cocreating what God hates.

We need to grasp one further concept as we consider our sin. We have discerned how closely God works with and in us. And so we need to ponder that every time we do an unloving act, a sinful act, we are, in a way, forcing God to do what God does not want to do. We can see how that is not loving. Anyone who does a grave sin is drawing God into cocreating what God hates. Well, as God is infinitely merciful, God is also infinitely just. The grave sinner runs the risk of provoking God's justice, of being dropped into *the great wine press of the wrath of God* (Rev. 14:19). Whatever that wine press might be, we'd better not be in it.

• • •

The first thing I must say about my sin is this: "I have sinned." Very many of us have sinned a lot, and perhaps grievously. But in my limited experience, most of us lack much sense of moral guilt, even though we have a corrosive sense that society is riddled with sin. We do not feel that *we* have offended God, but we do feel that the country is falling apart. We have trouble feeling unholy, though we may nurture a negative self-image and even sometimes hate ourselves. Nonetheless, we sin.

Only a few amazingly holy men and women seem never to have sinned grievously; they die, but death can't do to them what it does to the rest of us—some of their bodies remain intact for years, even decades. Bernadette Soubirous's body was still fresh more than 150 years after her death. St. Teresa of Ávila, St. Charles Borromeo, St. Jean Vianney, St. Francis Xavier, St. Madeleine Sophie Barat—their bodies remained intact a long time even though their coffins and their clothing had decayed.

That will not happen to me when I die. But on the way to death, I am a devout disciple, and I struggle against sin—my own sin. Here is what happens: I sin through my senses and in my own body: eating, drinking, narcissism in sexuality. I feel resentment rising from my bowels into my heart, and I cherish it. I find it amazingly easy to be slothful, wasting time on trivia. I'm saying the Our Father in the morning, get to "give us this day our daily bread," and I'm thinking that tonight we're going to have crawfish étouffée done with a real roux. Crawfish étouffée is not a sin in itself, but as a sauce on the Our Father?

The discerning disciple recognizes one reason we keep up this kind of thing, this sin: the body has its own memory. The ancient writers included this among the *relicta peccati*—those leftovers of sinning. The devout disciple takes a stand against these memories. When we fast during Lent, we are taking that stand. When we confront our habitual failures and when we generously give to those who need our help, we are taking that stand. Should it happen that we are not taking that stand against our flesh's memory, we will not long continue a maturely discerning life. We will be back to a life of conscience, fighting the world's sin as well as our own, needing the sacrament of reconciliation.

The discerning disciple also needs the sacrament of reconciliation, as Pope Francis has pointed out—and shown; remember the iconic photo of the white-clad pope plunking down in an ordinary confessional box to make his own confession. We disciples always need the sacrament of reconciliation. That God's mercy is the greatest of his works says a lot about God and even more about us: we need God to be, above all else, merciful. Because as long as we live, we will commit sins. St. Paul helps us here: *What a wretched man I am!* This from the thirteenth apostle whom Christ personally chose after his own resurrection! (Rom. 7:24).

We have to keep in mind that Jesus never promised that his disciples would not sin. He just said he would be with us always. And he is, in the Eucharist, "not a prize for the perfect but a powerful medicine and nourishment for the weak."[189] The pope is quoting St. Ambrose here, who gave all his wealth to the poor and lived a deeply holy life. This saint went on to write, "I must receive it always, so that it may always forgive my sins. If I sin continually, I must always have a remedy." The discerning disciple considers this. St. Ambrose always needed that remedy for his sins, and I think I don't?

38

Discernment, Conscience, and Compulsion

Even if the life of a person has been a disaster, even if it is destroyed by vices, drugs or anything else—God is in this person's life.

—Pope Francis

At some time during an ordinary life, everyone I know has had to handle hard habits. And sometimes we need to be aware that our culture tends to explain strong habits as compulsions or addictions—an explanation that at times gives us an excuse for sinful behavior or wrong thinking. And sometimes, in ordinary middle-class holy families, someone moves from discovering a fun drug to experimenting with it and then to habitually using it. With many drugs, habitual use becomes compulsive, and that leads to hopelessness. Some drugs cause severe addiction. Because the problem of addiction affects many lives, we do well to discern how we feel and think about it.

I heard a confession once in a very small town in one of the dozen states I have lived in as a priest. It was long ago, but it still haunts me. The man, call him Allan, was perhaps in his twenties, a burly working man. "My last confession," he began, "was a few days ago." After a pause, he blurted out that he had gone right back to what he had confessed: his addictions to alcohol and drugs. These led always to pornography and then to masturbation. He'd also stolen some electronic gear from a shop. He knew that all this was wrong and "not normal." I asked him gently to tell me what he meant, and he did. He felt that he had never had a chance to be normal. His alcoholic parents had fought. They had divorced loudly and angrily. He had had no love from his mother; his father had beat him. No family life at all. Now he had found someone to love. Allan and his fiancée had a baby together; they wanted to marry, but the woman's father wouldn't allow it. Allan respected the father but wished they could marry. He loved this woman.

Ending his silence, I told him that I thought I could hear repentance in his voice. He said in wrenching anguish, "*O God, yes!*" I gave him a penance and absolution. But I am afraid to think of how it ended, and I pray for them.

So, had he repented? After "a few days"? I thought, well, he repented as well as he was able, constrained as he was by the conviction that we become psychological slaves of substances and behaviors, our human freedom overwhelmed. He was bound up in these cultural forces—his soul as much poisoned by them as anyone's body is by salmonella in beef or lead in drinking water. The anguish in Allan's voice probably came as much from his feeling unfree and practically enslaved as from any moral sense of having offended God. But Allan knew how much he had offended love.

Allan, and many like him, need guidance to begin acknowledging responsibility for habits once deliberately embraced, now inveterate. He unquestionably needed therapy and other help. We show Christian hope by encouraging him to go to therapy or to a twelve-step program. But after that help is given and accepted, he will still need Christian help. He has a conscience, but it is straitjacketed in a culture that trammels us in the world, the flesh, and indeed in evil and does not know Christlife.[190]

In his first trip abroad as pope, Francis met with a group of recovering addicts in a Brazilian hospital. He had already visited two slums called *cracolandías*—"crack-lands," where drugs were the common exchange. He insisted that governments have to confront drug use, not dodge it by legalizing and taxing it. To these addicts—and to their loud applause—he blurted out, "You have to want to stand up; this is the indispensable condition!" He was able to say to this group that they "will find an outstretched hand ready to help you," which too many others do not find. He pleaded with the addicts that they not lose hope and told the rest of us: "Let us not rob others of hope, let us become bearers of hope!"[191]

What is the hope that mature disciples can hold out to those who want to break inveterate habits or compulsions or addictions? First, the hope of therapeutic help. We cannot argue habituated or addicted people into this hope.

We have to show it to them by our compassion that we believe this: "*Even if the life of a person has been a disaster, even if it is destroyed by vices, drugs or anything else—God is in this person's life*" (italics added).[192]

We hold out living *in union with Christ Jesus*—the *joy* of living in union with Christ, here and hereafter. In the meantime, and every day, we give by our own lives the witness of the joy of living Christlife with a good conscience—the joy of middle-class holiness. For we also believe what *Gaudium et Spes* declared: we have "in [our] heart a law [inscribed] by God," and conscience is our "most secret core and sanctuary," where we are alone with God.[193] But we are not naive about conscience. We recognize that "conscience must be informed and moral judgment enlightened," and that this "is a lifelong task."[194]

Part of that task for the mature disciple is to keep clear that much of what is now labeled addiction or compulsion was once called habit. Much of it should still be called habit. The clinical conditions are real, and we should courageously hold out to the addicted their need for therapy and, beyond therapy, the promise of living a joy we can witness to them. But our culture tends to use the words too loosely. By renaming many ordinary habits, our culture dims in us the sense of our moral responsibility for what we do. The discerning will see here one reason Americans find it hard to acknowledge their own sins.

To put it more vividly, our culture steals our freedom from us, the freedom to accept responsibility for what we do and, in so doing, to choose what we become. That theft is what Allan was suffering from when he made his confession. He wanted to be responsible for his actions, but he had been taught that he was addicted and compelled and therefore had no real freedom to quit alcohol and sex. He was what St. Paul lamented as being *a slave to sin.*

Our culture steals our freedom from us, the freedom to accept responsibility for what we do and, in so doing, to choose what we become.

And when we deal with people whose lives have been a disaster like Allan's—there are distressingly many in ordinary families now—we have to show them compassion. By our courtesy, refusal to be judgmental, and our patient kindness, we show what we believe in our hearts: that whatever our wretchedness and sins, *whenever our hearts condemn us*, we all cling to the sound hope of divine mercy, *for God is greater than our hearts, and knows everything* (1 John 3:20).

39

The Astonishing Joy of Humility

God always enters clothed in poverty, littleness.
—Pope Francis

The first experience of humility happens when I open my heart and contentedly say yes to my Creator. I then see in God's inexhaustible love the source of my being and the benevolent decision about who and what I am. This yes lays the foundation of mature discernment, which cannot go on without it.

It is a very concrete yes. I accept the place where God has put me, the time in which God creates me (which I did not exist to choose). I accept the real skills and qualities in my character (which I did not create but God is creating); I accept my parents (whom I did not choose but God chose); I accept my siblings (whom I did not select but God selected); I live content in the world's currents (which I cannot govern but God governs). In this mindset and heartset, I put God before all else—before all pleasures, profits, successes, and anything else in this world.

Then, of course, I falter and fail and sin. This creates—in God's infinite love and mercy—the occasion for discovering "the humility which is one of God's essential features, and which is part of God's DNA."[195] This is an astonishing thing to say, and it brings us up short. Who thinks of God as humble? But what else can we call a God who loves his chosen people, decade after decade and century after century—even when they do not love him back? Doesn't "humble" describe a God who has loved me into existence although I barely return his passionate personal love? A God who creates many, many hearts who willfully ignore him or proudly deny him? And a God who keeps on loving us.

This suffering love took on the flesh of those who did not love him back. We have to think that Jesus of Nazareth ought to have been exempt from the law of sin-and-death: he was, as the sinless Son of God. How could the consequence of sin touch him? Whether it could or not, Jesus made a decision to join us in our liability to death. *He was humbler yet, even to accepting death, death on a cross* (Phil. 2:8, NJB).

This is the humility of love. A person without spiritual maturity cannot comprehend this. The sinful will reject it as absurd. Humility clears the way for Jesus' disciples to learn to love, as we mature and our love grows to be like his in its deepest reality.

We accept who we are, not envious or jealous of anyone else. We recognize the gifts given us of intelligence, talent, and opportunity, and we enact those gifts. We will face trials and failures—even ones that threaten who we are. If we have humility like Jesus', we will embrace those trials and failures, humbly acknowledging *that suffering produces endurance, and endurance produces character, and character produces hope, and hope does not disappoint us, because God's love has been poured into our hearts through the Holy Spirit that has been given to us* (Rom. 5:3).

This is the way humility shapes a heart to put things in perspective and proper order. As we endure in love, we find ourselves having to yield, to reorder, to let go. A humble person is as content after yielding and letting go as when she gets what she preferred.

We accept who we are, not envious or jealous of anyone else. We recognize the gifts given us of intelligence, talent, and opportunity, and we enact those gifts.

A woman I will call Susan had just this experience. A professional woman of genuine accomplishment, she was working in a diocese and was eager to continue serving. But the Lord had other ideas. A man she knew only casually fell deeply in love with her and proposed to her, and she discovered that she wanted to love him and make a life together with him. That proved fairly easy at first because they both had faith in the sacrament of matrimony and their hearts were united. But the time came when Susan had to decide whether to continue her service in the diocese or to move with her spouse. She let go of her joyful service in the diocese, and they moved. She was surprised at how much joy she felt planning their new home and finding new ways to help people. This is the joy of humility.

Had she clung to her career, she would have been less humble. Clinging to what we have achieved when we are invited to move beyond it is one way to refuse the humility that will make us more Christlike. There are other ways to refuse, some quite obvious: I insist on having my own way, willfully, like a bridge partner who always moves the table a little bit—just a little bit, but *every time*. I can feverishly perform my prayers or my pious practices, as though forcing God's grace. I can be slothful, like the lazy teenager or the indolent adult watching hours of vacuous television. When changes happen in the Church, I can be rigid in wanting the liturgy to unfold as I have always known it and arrogant in feeling personally put upon when a new pastor changes it. In none of these situations am I humble.

When we become aware of attitudes like these and insist on protecting them, we are being proud. But pride always costs us. We will seem to be guarding a secret place in our heart that we are afraid to let God heal. "It is our hidden shame; it is the wound with which we torture ourselves," Pope Francis said about "the Hardening of Hearts."[196] To those who love us, this will seem to be a black hole in us, a silence they cannot penetrate and are afraid to test. So Pope Francis continues: "We see that space as our private domain, and we believe that only we need see it," but others do, and God does. We may feel humble, but we act proud.

The psalmist experienced this prideful sin: *While I kept silence, my body wasted away* (Ps. 32:3). As a humble believer, the psalmist knew that "God always enters clothed in poverty, in littleness."[197] So when we decide, *I will confess my offense to the Lord*, we find him waiting—eternally the patient, suffering Lover. And he will forgive the humbled heart.

This is the astonishing joy of humility as the psalmist discovered: *Happy the one whose offense is forgiven! Whose sin is remitted! O happy the one to whom the Lord imputes no guilt, in whose spirit is no guile.* For this spirit is humble, saying yes to God our Creator and *I confess* to our sins.

40

Discernment of Spirits

We need to distinguish clearly what might be a fruit of the kingdom from what runs counter to God's plan. This involves not only recognizing and discerning spirits, but also—and this is decisive—choosing movements of the spirit of good and rejecting those of the spirit of evil.

—Pope Francis

By the "fruit of the kingdom," Pope Francis means the enactments of loving and hope-filled designs—especially family life and care for all kinds of people who are in need.[198] This is the middle-class holiness that is establishing the reign of Christ here and now. And what is it that "runs counter to God's plan"? Pope Francis refers to the enactment of designs that do not establish Christ's reign. He sees them doing two other things: first, furthering earthly evolution, which will end in death, and second, establishing the spirit of evil in this moment of time.

The decisive moment comes not when we merely recognize the different spirits but on "choosing movements of the spirit of good and rejecting those of the spirit of evil."[199] St. Ignatius's "Rules for the Discernment of Spirits" help us do this.[200] Those rules make two basic distinctions: one between good spirit and evil spirits, and the other between consolation and desolation. This seems clear enough, and the substance of the rules can be stated briefly. But teasing out how they interrelate is as complex as a quadratic equation. The rules, after all, were written to help a spiritual director guide the full Spiritual Exercises, thirty dense days of intense prayer and penance. The Rules, nonetheless, offer some good norms to follow in reflecting on everyday life.

Start with the ones distinguishing good and evil spirits. A good spirit is one that brings thoughts and actions marked by peace, joy, and confidence.

It strengthens, encourages, and raises hope for the future. Just remember the thrilled crowds around Pope Francis in Baltimore in September 2015. The good spirit also keeps our feet on the ground, leading us to admit and repent our sins. If we weep, it's for joy and relief. This is *consolation*, which the good spirit gives to those who seriously follow Christ. We expect to live in consolation and Christ's joy.

An evil spirit does all the opposite of that, bringing thoughts and actions marred by doubt, desolation, and confusion. It leads to evil, as it did the people at Volkswagen, who now admit deliberately cheating by breaking laws about car exhaust fumes. Under a bad spirit, we feel weighed down and stuck in incessant problems and difficulties and not able to change.

This, understand, is *desolation*, not the "normal" condition of a follower of Christ. When I am in it, I forget to pray, don't feel at all holy—and don't ask for forgiveness. So when we are in desolation, we need to seriously check three things:

- Our consciences: are we sinning somehow?
- Our praise, reverence, and service of God: are we lazy and negligent?
- Our relationship with God: are our love and loyalty being tested?

The mature disciple will know what to do about any of these. And if it's the last one, the mature know to call on the gift of hope. "However dark things are, goodness always re-emerges and spreads."[201] That's one of the Rules: hold on in desolation. Relief will come.

A good spirit likes the light and is transparent and open. An evil spirit likes the dark and is deceitful and full of lies. And where a good spirit invites and gently encourages, the evil spirit stirs rancor and uses force. Sometimes, though, an evil spirit begins with an enticing good. That happened to a middle-aged man and woman who married, having waited a good while after their first spouses had died. Edgar (a name nothing like his real one) felt it was a good union, but one thing worried him. They each had separate incomes, and they had chosen to keep their money separate. He had felt that they made this accommodation in a good spirit. That's how things appeared, but pretty promptly the decision led to secrecy, a lot of deceit, and finally to rancorous fights. I had to tell him that it could not have been a good spirit moving them when what it led them to choose brought them to darkness and a cooling of their love. As happens with the influence of a bad spirit, though, Edgar did not feel free to change, and I don't know what happened to them after that.

Both spirits work in consolation as well as in desolation, though the good spirit means for us to go along in consolation, and the evil spirit urges us to move out of an apparent consolation into desolation. It's a good spirit that keeps Kurt, the dean of a college, calm when the faculty have their typically un-calm meetings.

Where a good spirit invites and gently encourages, the evil spirit stirs rancor and uses force.

Spiritual counselors offer other norms for dealing with consolation and desolation. For instance, we should remain grateful for consolation, because consolation is always a gift from God. And again, it's best that we stick to the good we are doing and have chosen when we get into desolation because desolation is not the time to change plans.

A very prayerful woman told me about an experience of discerning spirits. She had noticed a fellow worker doing something dishonest. She hated to share this with anyone. But in prayer she decided she had to tell the boss—which she hated even more. When she came to work that day, she began hesitating and doubting her decision. Then she promptly began to act impatient with everyone and to feel disgusted with her own work. She was mature enough to wait until this mood lifted and she could act in holiness, "choosing movements of the spirit of good and rejecting those of the spirit of evil."[202] That's discernment of spirits.

When we begin to notice how spirits move in us, we can trust our discernment of them to the extent that we are sure we are not being influenced by prejudice, attachment, selfishness, or egoism. This is mature discernment. We come to it through a life of self-mastery and prayer—and a lot of experience.

"With the eyes of faith," Francis wrote in one of his many summaries, "we can see the light which the Holy Spirit always radiates in the midst of darkness, never forgetting that '*where sin increased, grace has abounded all the more*'" (Rom. 5:20, italics added).[203]

Touchstones

- Sin-in-the-world is as real as diseases inherited in our DNA, and while humanity does make progress, we are still liable to sin.
- The world's sin is handed on to us and becomes sin-in-me, which we carry all our lives and must be saved from.
- Every one of us commits our own sins, even St. Paul the apostle, and we can feel ourselves suffering under these sins.
- Sin is a tremendous negative force in the world, but it will not obliterate the good God is creating. We live in hope.
- We see the reality of addiction and compulsion but also accept that sometimes we freely choose wrong.
- True humility grows in our saying yes to God creating us as he wishes us to be, and then enacting the gifts and graces he has chosen for us.
- No matter how far a person has gone into guilt and sin, God waits lovingly to forgive the repentant heart.
- The Eucharist is not a reward for holiness but a powerful help to live holy in Christ.

All the Saints and All Us Saints

Consider this "middle-class holiness" that Pope Francis sees all around him. If it's holiness we're looking at, what are we seeing?

- Holiness is a kind of uprightness, a being myself and being it well, as St. Francis de Sales said. I am content with who and what I am, not jealous of others and not condemning myself.
- Holiness is accepting that God is seeking me out, coming after me, pursuing me. I accept this—see it as a great gift, rejoice in it, and am not

afraid or resentful. For it is a powerful, unmanageable experience: God wants me, and I say my humble yes.

- Holiness means looking into Jesus' eyes and seeing two things: he loves me, he has singled me out; and he yearns for my love, for me to freely love him. I am astounded. I know that it's true.
- Holiness is acquiescing in this, and more, rejoicing in it—unafraid of where it will take me, very aware that it will set me to loving Jesus' other friends. And even his enemies.

For holiness allows us to stand in the Presence with interior peace and in patient passivity. I humbly accept that I belong in the Presence because I am summoned there. In that Presence, I act virtuously but do not strive for virtues, I simply and un-self-consciously radiate love, joy, peace, patience, kindness, goodness, trustfulness, gentleness, and self-control. This is simply the way the holy are—always penitent, always full of hope, our hearts full of faces and names.

Ultimately, the holy live in a communion we cannot create but the Holy Spirit pours into and among us.

PART NINE

DISCERNMENT AND CONSOLATION

41

Consolation and Human Flourishing

Faith also means believing in God, believing that he truly loves us, that he is alive, that he is mysteriously capable of intervening, that he does not abandon us and that he brings good out of evil by his power and his infinite creativity.
—Pope Francis

We Americans agree with our founders that citizens are "endowed by their Creator" with "unalienable Rights," among which is "the pursuit of Happiness."

The country's founders had faith in God and were living so as to enjoy eternity. Today, not too many of us are keen about eternity, but we all work along eagerly in "the pursuit of Happiness." A thoughtful person might wonder what happiness is. Some people, led by philosopher John Stuart Mill, are afraid to think about it. He wrote about a century after our independence that if you so much as ask yourself whether you are happy, you won't be.

Mature disciples do not fear thinking about happiness. Our faith is clear. We are created for joy, even as we go through "experiences of failure and the human weaknesses which bring so much pain."[204] For we have made the first great discernment: God momently creates and cares for us. And God, whose wisdom and power are infinitely greater than the evils that plague us, intends only good for us. So when we live this happiness, we are not being merely optimistic or progressive. We are being consoled—happy with the spiritual consolation given us by God's Holy Spirit.

We might look a little more closely into spiritual consolation because it includes our share of the world's happiness. Consolation and happiness, for instance, both concentrate on the present moment. Both stress the positive and reject what Aaron Beck called "distorted thinking" and a "negative self-image." Both aim at a sober assessment of human flourishing.[205]

Here is a wise listing of what constitutes human happiness:

- We enjoy plenty of positive experiences: good health, adequate income, and a sensible schedule.
- We engage with our gifts in good work and projects.
- We have good relationships both intimate and social, good ties that flow both ways (according to some recent, compelling studies, this factor is the single most reliable sign of happiness).
- We find meaning in our lives, setting ourselves to serve a great aspiration or enterprise.
- We are accomplishing goals that we have set for ourselves and remain determined to achieve them.[206]

This surely is authentic human happiness. And mature followers of Christ correctly ask God to grant it to us and to those we love. A retreatant once told me that he did not ask God for happiness because he thought that was being selfish and too attached to the world. I disagreed. I earnestly ask God to give me happiness right up until he takes me to himself, because that way I can witness to the joy of his mercy. I think this is just being prudent and wise.

But though the pursuit of happiness is common to all of us, mature Christians discern that, in the nonbeliever's pursuit, there is no room in it for the cross. The Becks and Seligmans, wise as they are, cannot integrate the cross into their "happiness." For them, it is the stumbling block. Yet every person alive will meet pain, suffering, and failure—it is simply the human condition.

The cross is not a stumbling block for us. We are given to understand suffering and failures as the cross in our everyday lives. We remain a joyful people because, first of all, we are given the faith and hope that God "brings good out of evil by his power and his infinite creativity." At a deeper level, we remain happy even in hardship and pain because we believe that God "truly loves us, that he is alive, that he is mysteriously capable of intervening, that he does not abandon us," not ever.[207] The power of accepting these truths and believing them with all our heart—this begins to describe, not the happiness that all Americans pursue, but *spiritual consolation.*

Consolation begins deep in the self that is grateful to God in all things. As G. K. Chesterton once explained, gratitude is happiness magnified by wonder. Jesus' act at Cana shows how practical gratitude is: in the first place, Jesus intended his friends to be happy and have a good time. He and his mother came to this wedding party to enjoy it. When that enjoyment was threatened, Jesus felt impelled (with a little help from his mother) to show what his disciples could expect: first of all, more wine. They enjoyed the wine, and then they understood the sign: Jesus had *revealed his glory; and his disciples believed in him* (John 2:11). That is consolation. In everyday life, we feel joy in whatever comes. For whatever comes arrives in the context of God's overarching care: *the earth has yielded its produce; God, our God has blessed us* (Ps. 67:6, NJB).

Well, we don't have parties every day, so how do we experience consolation in everyday life? We feel it in the easy flow of faith and hope and love—head and heart and hands—as we go about doing the next good thing. Consolation keeps us feeling that we are enough and that our life is enough. It lets us sleep well and wake refreshed. We do not fret about whether we are doing God's will or not. We are not anxious that the world might suddenly end. This hope-filled mind and a quiet heart flow into doing the next good thing even when it is hard or repulsive. For instance, we go to the polls and vote when no candidate is flawless—and we vote with quiet mind.

Consolation begins deep in the self that is grateful to God in all things. As G. K. Chesterton once explained, gratitude is happiness magnified by wonder.

Consolation also comes to us in prayer. On ordinary days we have a fixed time and place to pray, perhaps with the day's readings. Just managing to keep at this spiritual habit is a consolation. Keeping our attention on God and the things of God is a consolation. And even if we spend time in silence and quiet without thinking much, just being there enacts our belief that God lives, truly loves us, "is mysteriously capable of intervening, that he does not abandon us."[208]

Then, on a Sunday, we feel ready to go to church, and the Mass doesn't seem all that long (well, maybe the homily). At family dinner (it's a consolation if we can continue having family dinner in this fractured time), we may feel a rush of happy affection when one of the younger family members leads us in saying grace.

This calls attention to what we started with: consolation *includes* happiness, and for this reason we sometimes get them mixed up. At the family meal, for instance, consolation comes mixed with the fragrance of good food and family love. We can confuse plain human enjoyment with spiritual consolation, as Jesus had to point out to some of his disciples. After he had multiplied loaves, they came looking for him, and he had to tell them, *Very truly, I tell you, you are looking for me, not because you saw signs, but because you ate your fill of the loaves* (John 6:26). They did not believe in him, which would have been a spiritual consolation; they wanted to be filled with bread, which is human happiness. So Jesus taught them. *Do not work for the food that perishes, but for the food that endures for eternal life, which the Son of Man will give you* (John 6:27).

One of our greatest consolations is believing in Christ's presence in the Eucharist. Strengthened by that food, we convert the ordinary happiness of the world into something more. For our happiness "entails gratitude and gratuitousness, a recognition that the world is God's loving gift, and that we are called quietly to imitate his generosity in self-sacrifice and good works."[209] This is consolation, the magnanimity full of the joy that we are living in union with Christ Jesus.

42

God Consoles His People

The Holy Spirit works as he wills, when he wills and where he wills; we entrust ourselves without pretending to see striking results.
—Pope Francis

The Holy Spirit momently attends to every single person alive, even to the jihadist and the dope-ridden derelict. But the Spirit most surely gives special attention to those who have accepted Jesus as their Lord. He makes the joy of Jesus penetrate into our spiritual lives like a leaven. The tradition has called this "consolation," since the psalmist rejoiced, *When the cares of my heart are many, your consolations cheer my soul* (Ps. 94:19).

We have to be sure we understand how the Spirit moves in those who live a discerning life. For spiritual consolation is the easy continuance in a life of grace that is basically good. In the paintings of saints, it's a holy glow. But in fact, just accepting, on a dull workday morning, that God has made me holy is, in itself, a spiritual consolation.

Consolation continues as we live the virtues that the Spirit has endowed us with, beginning with faith, hope, and love. These virtues energize other gifts the Spirit gives us: emotionally (courage, piety); affectively (understanding, counsel); and intellectually (knowledge, fear of the Lord); and charge our head, heart, and hands with wisdom. And as we continue doing the next good thing, we are enacting these virtues with God's grace.

Note in passing: if we deliberately acted against our conscience and sinned, the Spirit would withdraw consolation and leave us without it—like turning the air conditioning off on a really hot day. Consolation is God's gift; we do not earn it.

Ignatian spirituality connects consolation with discernment. Pope Francis and many others learn this connection when they make the Spiritual

Exercises of St. Ignatius. But we keep mindful that mature disciples are discerning all the time, and the Spirit is consoling us all the time—empowering our grasp of the *faith*, our heartfelt *believing*, and our *enactments* in grace.

First, faith. Consolation affects our faith by bringing clarity about what has been revealed by God, and sureness about our understanding it. I found a good example of this in a wealthy retired businessman I'll call Don. He collected unsold bread from dozens of grocers and delivered it to the diocese's soup kitchen. He had been doing this on Tuesdays and Fridays for more than twenty years when I last talked with him. Don kept this clear: *as you did it to one of the least of these who are members of my family, you did it to me* (Matt. 25:40). He lived in the consolation of having this truth crystal clear: he was feeding Christ. That gave him the fortitude and perseverance to keep at what he was doing for years and years.

When we are in consolation, we remember just those truths of faith that are pertinent to us right now. Even if we are struggling or hurting, we remain clear about the truth that matters at this moment. For one middle-aged man—call him Warren—the truth that mattered was this: "The love of the spouses requires, of its very nature, the unity and indissolubility of the spouses' community of persons, which embraces their entire life: 'so they are no longer two, but one flesh.'"[210]

Warren's wife was highly intelligent and very gifted. They had been married a dozen years when I met them. They loved each other deeply. Then she began ricocheting through emotional states and bizarre behaviors. Warren had good work, but hard work. Yet when his wife became very sick, he cared for her day after day until she died of a brain tumor. I could see how his faith gave him a great heart. He needed it: when his spouse died, he was truly bereft for a long while.

Second, belief. Consolation affects our hearts, our believing. Most notably, it makes us magnanimous, which means "being able to appreciate the small things inside large horizons, those of the kingdom of God."[211] We see God working all through his great creation, and we "look at the horizon from the position where we are," as Pope Francis put it. Looking up like this helps us "to do the little things of every day with a big heart open to God and to others."[212] So Warren had shopped and cooked and cleaned, day after day, always aware of the horizon of a love like the Holy Trinity's.

Consolation warms and strengthens our hearts. It helps move faith from head to conviction and commitment. Donald Gelpi, Jesuit priest-philosopher and theologian, was invited into the Charismatic movement as it began in New Orleans in the early 1970s. His way of thinking was very philosophical, but he found himself deeply attracted to charismatic prayer (which is not notably philosophical).

He told me that during one evening's long prayer service, he had begun to feel very uncomfortable because the group began noisily praising God in tongues. Then he remembered that he had committed himself to believing that the "Holy Spirit works as he wills, when he wills and where he wills."[213] When he remembered that, Donald told me, his discomfort evanesced. Years after that, he sometimes fell into "tongues" when we prayed together, and that prayer proved a consolation to him until the day he died in 2011.[214]

Consolation warms and strengthens our hearts. It helps move faith from head to conviction and commitment.

Finally, enactment. Consolation brings about the work of our hands. Donald Gelpi's experience demonstrates the way consolation affects what we do and how we do it. We feel confident that we are doing what God wants done. We just calmly get on with it; we do the next good thing with a quiet mind and heart. Mature disciples have long thought, and Ignatian spirituality emphasizes, that living consoled after a decision gives us a good sign that God is pleased with our choice.

This was clearly the experience of the Jesuit journalist whose interview with Pope Francis appeared in Jesuit journals worldwide. As he told about it, Fr. Antonio Spadaro was asked to wait in an anteroom when he went to the Casa Santa Marta. Sitting there, he felt himself more than a bit anxious. Of course he is—he's going to question the pope! Then he remembered the meeting of Jesuit editors who had floated the idea of the interview. They weighed it, discussed it, and made a prayerful discernment. The questions were not his own, and the Spirit gave him a confident feeling that they "would express everyone's interests."[215] They certainly have, and his confident feeling doing the interview shows how consolation works.

For spiritual consolation is a grace—the Holy Spirit working in our whole self. It is not merely a passing emotion and a good feeling. It is the longer experience that God is good and that all he creates is good—including each of us and every single thing we experience apart from sin.

43

Consolation Is Doing God's Will

I encourage you to rejoice with those who rejoice, and to weep with those who weep; to ask God for a heart capable of compassion, to bend over the wounds of the body and the spirit and to take to many people the consolation of God.
—Pope Francis

We might tend to think that the gift of Jesus' *joy to the full* means that consolation is first of all having a heart full of good feeling. But at its most enduring, consolation is rooted not in our hearts but in our hands. It is the doing of what God gives us to do. *For we are what he has made us, created in Christ Jesus for good works, which God prepared beforehand to be our way of life.*[216]

When we do not do God's will, the Spirit withdraws consolation. This is why those who live in sin—ignoring God, stealing and piling up wealth selfishly, casually fornicating—live spiritually desolate even when their lives are glutted with pleasure and power and they appear to be very happy.

But when we set ourselves to live well, the Spirit gives us confidence that "I am doing what God wants done"—and acting in that confidence is consolation. The mature disciple roots this confidence in the heartfelt belief that God the Lord is still creating me, moment by moment, with an infinite and eternal love. We root it in the truth that Jesus Christ takes me as his own each time I receive him in communion. Fortified with this, we do God's will not only in our big choices but also in "the gray pragmatism of the daily life of the Church, in which all appears to proceed normally."[217] We can get worn down and become small-minded, focused only on the "passing things" that the prayers for Lent in the new liturgy urge us to care about less than the things of eternity.

> The mature disciple roots this confidence in the heartfelt belief that God the Lord is still creating me, moment by moment, with an infinite and eternal love.

To continue discerning, we need to remain aware of a broader horizon. We have long been connecting consolation with prayer and making major choices in life. We may not have been discerning that the Spirit is *always* consoling us. But St. Ignatius points out that any time we experience deeper faith or hope and greater love, the Spirit is indeed consoling us.

Whenever we enact our knowledge that Jesus is Lord and give him attention and ask for his help, we are consoled. When we enact our belief that he has called us to recognize sins and repent of them—and to forgive them—we are consoled. We enact his command to love one another—and when we can do that with spouse, children and parents, friends, and even enemies, magnanimously, that greatness of spirit is consolation. And his Spirit of love guides us to enact our gifts of wisdom, prudence, fortitude, and the rest—becoming authentically the people God wishes us to become.

We usually appreciate consolation most readily in the psychological terms of how we feel about things. But the more fundamental and enduring consolation is doing what I am doing, confident that it is what God wants done. God's will is not some esoteric treasure that only those singled out by the Spirit have the call and ability to seek. It's not the jewel merchant finding one humongous pearl (see Matt. 13:45). No, God's will steadily charges everything going on around me and in me all the time. When any of us acts as if we believe that and persevere in doing the next good thing, we live in consolation—a consolation that should fill all of us through the most ordinary of days.

• • •

True, some of us have been singled out for notable and great vocations, as was St. Teresa of Calcutta. She presents a clear case of the consolation of doing what God wants done, even when prayer and spiritual experience are dark. St. Teresa famously wrote to a spiritual guide: "Jesus has a very special love for you. . . . As for me, the silence and the emptiness is so great, that I look and do not see—Listen and do not hear."[218] These words were quoted over and over again in the world press and were constantly misunderstood. Some agnostics thought that she was one of them. Some Christians feared that she was somehow a fake.

But men and women who understand these experiences—full disclosure: I don't count myself among them—point out that she was experiencing what St. John of the Cross calls a *dark night*—a mysteriously great, suffering consolation of divine love. But we do not need to understand that to understand Mother Teresa's deepest stream of consolation: she was doing what God wanted done. And visibly, she was able "to rejoice with those who rejoice, and to weep with those who weep," and God gave her "a heart capable of compassion, to bend over the wounds of the body and the spirit and to take to many people the consolation of God."[219]

In her heart and in her head, St. Teresa's consolation was the profound confidence that God wanted her to witness to Jesus Christ by working with the poorest of the poor. "We may not always be able to reflect adequately the beauty of the Gospel, but there is one sign which we should never lack: the option for those who are least, those whom society discards."[220] St. Teresa never lacked that sign; she gave it all around the world.

To know unshakably what God wants me to do, what God wants to do with me and through me, is the greatest of all human consolations. Jesus of Nazareth lived in this consolation; as he said, *the Son can do nothing on his own, but only what he sees the Father doing; for whatever the Father does, the Son does likewise* (John 5:19).

This consolation—knowing how to be and to move as confidently as steel filings know to move toward a magnet—can hardly be overestimated, and esteeming it is the epitome of discernment. It is living with certainty that God continues to create me and my world. It is accepting the things I must do—shunning the sinful—as God's passionate love shaping me for eternal life. This consolation is what keeps husband and wife married through "richer and poorer, in sickness and in health," rearing children in difficult times. It was the consolation of a woman who laughingly answered a question about her vexing spouse: "Divorce him? No. Sometimes I could kill him. But divorce him? No."

The sacrament of matrimony is more than what American culture calls marriage. It is the grace of knowing that a personal love that is blessed by Christ's Church brings us into a communion with the Blessed Trinity—a union that is somehow emphasized with each child born to a couple. That couples endure joblessness, willful teenagers, cancer of breast or prostate, and are still loving on their thirty-fifth anniversary—that is a miracle of grace, and their enduring fidelity is the crowning consolation of their lives and selves.

Men are downsized, women are underemployed, and couples are sterile or impotent. Elderly religious watch their congregations change and die. Yet the mature disciple calmly and hopefully does the next good thing, acting on what Jesus said: *Do not let your hearts be troubled. Believe in God, believe also in me* (John 14:1). When we just get on doing what we know God wants us to do, we may not feel like it, but we know with deep certainty that we are infinitely loved.

44

Discerning Mature Experiences of Consolation

Joy adapts and changes, but it always endures, even as a flicker of light born of our personal certainty that, when everything is said and done, we are infinitely loved.

—Pope Francis

After the bombing of Pearl Harbor on December 7, 1941, the Japanese clamped down on missionaries in their country. Quite promptly, Jesuit Father Pedro Arrupe, who would later become head of the Jesuit order, was jailed on suspicion of espionage. He was kept in miserable solitary confinement as Christmas neared. In this dark loneliness one night, Father Arrupe heard people gathering outside his cell. He wondered if the time of his execution had come.

"Suddenly," he wrote after the war, "there arose a soft, sweet, consoling Christmas carol, one of the songs which I had myself taught to my Christians. I was unable to contain myself. I burst into tears. They were my Christians who, heedless of the danger of being themselves imprisoned, had come to console me."[221] Father Arrupe already knew that "joy adapts and changes, but it always endures," even after harsh treatment by Vatican officials and a totally debilitating stroke. He lived the truth that "when everything is said and done, we are infinitely loved."[222]

We all know the sweetness of Christmas carols, and it illustrates a point that St. Ignatius made about how the Spirit works. In mature disciples, he found, the good spirit moves "sweetly, lightly, and gently," rather like the Christmas carol. He found another simile for how the good spirit moves that has become famous: the good spirit comes into the good heart gently "like a drop of water falling on a sponge."[223]

Inspirations to do the right thing, of course, can also be hard. We can experience feelings of repugnance or even anger at something we have to do. Not long ago, I had to confront a friend who was saying hard things about the president. When I thought about it beforehand, an ugly feeling rose in me, along with the thought that he was too immature and should recognize his slander. He needed, my clenched fist suggested, some tough handling. That harsh thought hit my heart like a drop of water hitting a stone (St. Ignatius's other waterworks image). A movement of this kind comes from a bad spirit, whose inspirations are characteristically harsh and abrade our calm. Satan loves violence. So I "asked God for a heart capable of compassion" and cooled it for a while, and the conversation went surprisingly well.[224]

The Holy Spirit loves gentleness and calm. A deeply spiritual friend wrote a while back that she wished she had clearer notions about consolation. "I have been waking up and going through the day in what I can only call 'contemplation in action.'" She said this was not the deep, almost passive, contemplation of prayer. It was "just a powerful feeling of refreshment and delight in the presence and action of the Holy Trinity." This consolation has been part of middle-class holiness since it was urged by the French Carmelite Brother Lawrence, who died in 1691.[225]

The Spirit moves in earth's beauty, too. When he was an undergraduate at Harvard, Avery Dulles experienced the Spirit's gentleness in nature. During college, he had left the faith of his Presbyterian forebears and didn't believe in God at all. One spring morning, though, he was strolling along the river Charles when his eye fell on the branches of a shrub with their tips turning green. It was life returning. He wrote later—he had become a Jesuit and a cardinal—that he had suddenly known in his whole self that there is a great something—or someone—behind this return of life, and he knew, with a kind of warming in his heart, that he was to go and find him. That is spiritual consolation, entirely typical of the actions of the Holy Spirit, the kind of action many of us experience.

Mature consolation does not always come in an idea or feeling, though. Sometimes it comes in the shape of a concrete decision. We can make a decision to do some good almost without recognizing that we are about to do it. St. Ignatius considers this an important grace: "When God our Lord so moves and attracts the will that a devout soul without hesitation, or the possibility of hesitation, follows what has been manifested to it."[226] He gives as instances the decision of Levi to follow Jesus; this event, depicted in Caravaggio's painting, moved Cardinal Archbishop Bergoglio at a key moment in his life. And then there's the conversion of Saul of Tarsus. But some are much less dramatic, as was the sudden decision of a fast-food employee to get a college education. She had to go through the hoops but never backed off her sudden decision, which has proven a great benefit to her young family.

Mature consolation does not always come in an idea or feeling, though. Sometimes it comes in the shape of a concrete decision.

This kind of undramatic work of consolation is illustrated in the story of Whitney Belprez. She grew up in a vaguely religious family, but by the time she was in high school, she was agnostic. She writes that she somehow dated a lot of Catholic men, most of them Canadian-Americans. In college she had discovered an interest in world religions and majored in religious studies. She and one of the Catholic men became serious and went to visit his family. Whitney found herself charmed by their simple enactment of their religion. One thing, however, she was certain of: she would not become Catholic. They married, she began attending Mass, but this stayed clear: she would not become a Catholic. It was a decision.

Then the Holy Spirit moved. "Within days of making the decision to not enter the Church I woke up one morning and knew that God was inviting me to become Catholic—I knew it like I know that I love my daughter." The consolation was a decision to enact faith and hope and love of God. "It was the most real, physical feeling I had on my heart and felt in my whole body" she wrote. She did not know how to explain it, but "I knew with my entire being what God was asking of me."[227] We think of that clarity, that deep conviction of the next good thing to do, as spiritual consolation.

The gift of a decision is not always unexpected and without precedent, though. It can come as ordinary days and years pass by, consolation day by day.

My mother, for instance, had in mind being a nun until she saw my father. I have found in more than fifty years of priesthood that their story is common enough among Catholic couples. My mother told me that she came to know without doubt that she wanted to marry this college football player. Their marriage had rough spots as they raised five children born in four years and eight months in the depths of the Great Depression. They chose over and over again to let their vows remain the trellis on which their selves grew and branched, were directed and constrained, until death did them part. I suggest that we consider those repeated choices the most fundamental of consolations.

It truly is one of the marvels of the middle-class holiness all around us.

Touchstones

- Spiritual consolation has many of the qualities of human happiness.
- Human happiness comes with having good health and enough wealth, good relationships, and good work, especially in some great project or human cause.
- Consolation is a gift of the Holy Spirit and is the normal state of a faithful disciple. It is not mainly a feeling but a way of living.
- The happiness of the unbelieving world around us cannot abide suffering. But Christians are consoled in our suffering by our trust in God in Christ.
- The discerning disciple knows that consolation gives us clarity of faith, firmness of hope in our hearts, and confidence that we are doing God's will.
- Enacting the graces of matrimony through long years is a sign of a deep spiritual consolation.

- In fact, total confidence that I am doing with my life what God wants in me is the most enduring and firm consolation.
- The Holy Spirit surprises us with consolations, sometimes moving others to console us, sometimes just breaking in on our spirits and lifting or convincing them.

The Consolation of Encountering Jesus Christ

Pope Francis, right at the beginning of his exhortation, invites us "to a renewed personal encounter with Jesus Christ." And he adds, "I ask all of you to do this unfailingly each day."* The pontiff's personal experience is glaringly obvious: he loves Jesus Christ with a personal love, and he knows that Jesus Christ loves him. We all need that intimate consolation.

For a thousand years and more, mature disciples have opened themselves to encountering Jesus by praying with the Gospels. The classical method, *Lectio Divina*, moves the person from reading to meditating and then through praying to contemplation. This is the way monks and nuns prayed for centuries, and the way many laymen and women are now praying who are able and want to spend a long time in daily mental prayer.

Another method of prayer is a lot like this but with differences that make it an effective way for disciples to pray who lead ordinary, busy lives. It also has four steps.

- *Lectio*: We might read the Scriptures assigned for the day's liturgy. We might also have to attend to some item on the day in our calendar, or to something going on in our home or in the world. We read until something stands out.
- *Consideratio*: This prayer is what Jesus did when he considered the lilies of the field and the birds of the air. He compared things. He held them up and inspected them from various perspectives. He thought about their story and the conditions of their lives. Consideration weaves together world and Word.
- *Oratio*: While thinking and pondering in God's Presence, we are regularly called to thanksgiving and to the prayer of petition. We thank God for everything and for special things. We ask for help and we ask for what we

want, as Jesus instructed us to do. We beg for help. We commit ourselves to keep finding what God hopes for in us and in our lifeworld.

- *Discernimento*: In the busy life, finding God acting in the world, the last stage of this *Lectio Divina* is not quiet contemplation but busy judgment and decision. This prayer will lead to action—to the enactment of the faith and hope and love that we have experienced in our time of prayer.

This is the *lectio divina cotidiana*—"quotidian" referring to ordinary days of everyday life. This is the prayer that helps busy mature disciples grow into a *contemplative attitude*. The daily prayer is, itself, a great consolation.

*Pope Francis, *The Joy of the Gospel*, para. 3.

PART TEN

DISCERNMENT AND DESOLATION

45

Discerning the Experience of Desolation

What we propose then, is precisely a militant hope. To understand the process of discernment that such hope requires, we do well to consider the despairing attitudes that every so often take root in our souls.

—Arbp. Jorge Mario Bergoglio

Ignatius Loyola began to live a "militant hope" to serve God and his Lady Mary like a soldier conquering enemy territory: himself.[228] All too promptly, he felt a "despairing attitude" take root in his soul. He had fasted to the ruination of his digestive system and prayed as though he were assaulting God. This raw spiritual crusader made himself so desperate and distraught that he stood at the edge of suicide. That despairing attitude brought him up short. This can't be the Holy Spirit, he knew, who does not want our ruination but our flourishing. Ignatius learned a lot about hope and desolation.

Anyone serious about discernment needs that hope and also needs to know what desolation is and does. We see plenty of it in our culture. But, like our non-Christian friends, we ordinarily brand it *depression.* Some depression is a clinical health problem, and we have to acknowledge it and deal with it. That's not the subject here. But many experiences we label depression are less psychological than spiritual. Depression might be ended by therapy, but desolation is ended by discernment and hope. To get hold of this, we might start the way Ignatius started, considering "the despairing attitudes that every so often take root in our souls."[229]

What are these "despairing attitudes"? At their extremes, they include thoughts of suicide, which ends more lives in the United States than do car accidents.[230] But unless we are afflicted with a clinical depression, mature disciples are very unlikely to suffer thoughts of suicide. Mostly, we suffer from just being down, discouraged, and disheartened—that is, desolate.

St. Ignatius came to see that at its core, desolation is diminished faith, dimmed hope, and cold love. When no revealed truth of faith throws light on our experience right now, we are in desolation. When we wallow along with an empty heart and feel no special hope for what is to come, we are in desolation. When we do not much care about doing the next good thing but are "wholly slothful, tepid, sad, and as if separated from our Creator and Lord," we are in desolation.[231] Becoming mired in self-pity, being lured to resentments, losing interest in the prayer we've been keen on, and paying no attention to Jesus Christ after receiving him in communion—all of these are examples of desolation.

You could say that desolation numbs us, causing our appreciative awareness of the graced, vital flow among head and heart and hands to dim or go out altogether. Desolation is a sort of spiritual anesthesia. Is it important to discern whether we're in spiritual desolation? Yes, it's quite important, because we can expect that we are being tested one way or another:

St. Ignatius came to see that at its core, desolation is diminished faith, dimmed hope, and cold love.

- Head—the faith is no longer relevant: What is truth?
- Heart—closed in on self, cold, diffident: What's to hope for?
- Hands—enjoying pleasures or just "doing things": Go shop!

Start with the test of faith. Desolation comes when we do not think that any revealed truth is relevant to the experiences we are going through. It happens to people living the sacrament of matrimony, which spiritually challenges cultural norms.[232]

Elizabeth Moulin is a colleague (we taught together at Perkins School of Theology in SMU) who assesses cases for annulment. With graduate degrees in counseling and long experience in spirituality, she can judge that many people who seek annulments never understood the sacrament of marriage to begin with. She told me about an honest, charming couple who married very young. They had gone through a Catholic wedding, really just doing what nice people do. They had had no appreciative awareness that their covenanted love witnessed to the faithful love of the Triune God. Their ignorance exiled them to the desert of "marriage problems" that would not yield to psychosocial solutions in marriage counseling. Once past the first joys of married life, they lived a long desolation that turned tensions and disappointments into dissatisfaction with themselves and their married life. They ended it with divorce.

This raises the test of our heart. Desolation obviously tangles up our hearts' affections and desires. This is a special challenge for Americans because, as Francis wrote, "The culture of prosperity deadens us." Let's face it: we live mostly as exuberant consumers. Our cultural economy effectively invites us to "the idolatry of money"—or as the pontiff's Spanish has it, to *feticismo*, making a fetish of money.[233] When I feel disoriented and down, I sometimes just feel like going out and buying something—anything.

When I use money and things to assuage my desolation, I am giving in and actually embracing my desolation. Americans rarely consider that piling up new things is a form of desolation. But it is. It sets us up to be self-centered and greedy and to become blind and deaf to the ways our consumerist economy is enriching some people to unhealthy excess and leaving others without work and in poverty. "Almost without being aware of it, we end up being incapable of feeling compassion at the outcry of the poor, weeping for other people's pain, and feeling a need to help them, as though all this were someone else's responsibility and not our own."[234] For a follower of Christ, that incapacity is a serious desolation.

There's desolation in our hands—our actions. When mature disciples do not recognize desolation, we enact that confusion and nescience. Margaret showed me that. She is a religious woman whose ministry is in higher education. At one point, she was handling serious conflicts in her college ministry and tensions in her religious community. Margaret's language is always vivid, but once she was almost eloquent; she felt disheartened, too discouraged to pray, distant from her sister religious and disaffected from a ministry she had long enjoyed. The problems she detailed were real problems. So was the desolation, though she did not call it that.

She was having no trouble in her faith in Christ and the sacraments. She did not doubt God's love and care for her. So we turned to what she actually was doing. There, roots of desolation were clearly evident in her actions. She was spending time at the college doing nothing much, just getting away from her community's problems. She ignored the diet her health required. And forgot prayer.

The things she was doing were all clear signs of spiritual desolation. But Margaret did not identify what she was experiencing as "darkness of soul" or "turmoil of spirit," which is what St. Ignatius calls them.[235] And who would think to call just pleasantly wasting time, with things to munch on and sip, in very nice surroundings, "being inclined to the low and earthly"? We wouldn't; Ignatius did.

What helped me see what she was going through were the vivid adjectives she had in fact used: disheartened, discouraged, disaffected, and distanced. Her names for her desolate experiences all began with *dis-*. After this encounter with Margaret, I began reviewing my notes on desolations from earlier conferences and materials I'd read. Similar words kept coming up: *disinterest, distress, distraction, disaffection, disappointment, dissatisfaction, disgust, discouragement.* We postmoderns seem to experience desolation when we are somehow dissed. Perhaps it is worth looking at this.

46

Desolation Is Now Living Dissed

In the cross is the history of the world: grace and sin, mercy and repentance, good and evil, time and eternity.
—Pope Francis

The word *dissed* began as athletic slang. Players are dissed by teammates, friends, or coaches when they are disdained, disregarded, and perhaps dismissed from a team.[236]

But the sharp athletic slang describes well a lot of what we experience off courts and fields. Most Americans are discouraged at the way our nation is going. The middle class is disappointed with the economy. Being dissed is almost a sign of our times. The discerning disciple interprets this as a spiritual desolation.

Being dissed seems to happen so often that it could be the name of our daily cross. Consider how many daily experiences begin with *dis-*.

- We read the morning paper and are *disgusted* with gridlock politics and *distorted* news reporting.
- The young are *distracted* all day with cell phones, and the rest of us with busyness and errands.
- We feel *distressed* about parents with dementia and about *dysfunction* in our families.
- Too many of us "feel *disillusioned* and no longer identify with the Catholic tradition," to put it in Pope Francis's typically mild words.[237]
- Who can sleep easy who is *disappointed* or even *dismayed* by the shrinking reach of income?

These experiences wear away our faith, hope, and love. They are temptations in the form of desolation. But since we don't recognize them when they hit, we end up *living* dissed.

Angela, a prayerful spouse and mother of grown children, is a spiritual director and organizer with a discerning heart. But Angela lives dissed. One day she e-mailed me, and I noticed several *disses* glaring out of the e-mail. She recently had experiences that puzzled her. She was aware of a solid faith in Christ and a deep Christian hope. She was keeping up a lot of good work. But she felt *distracted* all day long as she juggled family, prayer, and spiritual work. Sometimes she felt simply *distraught*. She was troubled because her prayer was dry, and she just felt *disconnected* from Jesus Christ. She knew she was beloved of God and loved God in her turn, yet she lived vaguely *discontented* all the time. She did not know what to make of it.

She knew that she had to find the right side of "grace and sin, mercy and repentance, good and evil, time and eternity."[238] But she needed to ask what all those disses were about: distracted, distraught, disconnected, discontented. What was putting her among the disciples Jesus challenged for not *using their eyes to see, using their heart to understand, changing their ways and being healed by me*? (John 12:40, NJB). What was behind that and needed the healing of God's grace—head or heart or hands?

- **Head?** Was she remembering that God is creating her in this moment and mindful that God cares that she works with him—or was she too distracted?
- **Heart?** Did she hold in her heart that God loves her as she is but loves her too much to leave her as she is—or was she focused on herself and dissatisfied with her life?
- **Hands?** Was she doing the next good thing and leaving the rest in God's hands—or was she dissipating her energies by not prioritizing and then getting distraught to have to leave so much undone?

When we recognize this kind of experience in our day-to-day lives, we are not likely to call it desolation. Angela did not. We are more likely to call it depression (which she wondered about) or blame it on negative self-image or compulsion or addiction (she thought maybe she was a workaholic). But these experiences are spiritual experiences of desolation that sting and hinder us as we try to *lead a quiet and peaceable life in all godliness and dignity* (1 Tim. 2:2).

Being dissed was a passing experience for Angela. It ended more quickly than did her dislike of the new English liturgy. Unhappily, for many mature Christians, being dissed lasts a lot longer. If we let it last, we can come to live as we heard Pope Francis describe, "overcome by chronic discontent and by a listlessness that parches the soul."[239] This discontent is spiritual desolation. Worse than just making us feel bad, it makes us liable to any number of temptations.

Consider, for instance, what living dissed did to one mature and discerning Christian man. Justin worked in a shrinking corporation. He was between assignments and disappointed that his new assignment was long in coming. He constantly felt *disillusioned* with the company (bought out and gutted) and *distrusted* his boss (with some good reason). One afternoon, a colleague casually groused that their office was in its usual shambles. It was a routine office complaint, but Justin's reaction was not routine. "I blasted him," he told me. "I totally blasted him. I lost it. I hadn't lost my temper in a long, long time." But he had let being *disillusioned* and *distrusting* of his company get to him. Being *disappointed* in himself and *disagreeing* sharply with his colleague, he gave in to the sin of a wounding anger.

What mature disciples of the Lord, like Angela and Justin, are dealing with is a low-grade postmodern desolation. In my limited experience, very few of us American Catholics escape it.

Living dissed is a sign of our times that we have a "grave responsibility" to interpret.[240] In the new millennium, we Americans are discouraged by the disarray of our politics and disgusted with ugly political ads. We are too busy to listen to the Church's social teaching. We put up with legislation "linked to disillusionment and the crisis of ideologies," and we neglect voting, even though our bishops have

What mature disciples of the Lord, like Angela and Justin, are dealing with is a low-grade postmodern desolation.

declared it a sacred duty.[241] Our technological culture has so leeched the wonder and awe out of nature and has so mismanaged natural resources that we hardly feel reverence for God's creation. And popular culture has so debased sexuality that we hardly feel dismayed with explicit ads in print and the grossly sexualized themes and characters in films and on television.

We are faced with this: living dissed can set off "processes of dehumanization which would then be hard to reverse"—cynicism, depression, faithlessness.[242] It is one hinge of our struggle with "grace and sin, mercy and repentance, good and evil, time and eternity."[243] Those among us who deal with it successfully pray, read, and have good friends with whom we can share our experiences. We also know that every desolation opens us to temptation.

We beg daily that God "lead us not into temptation." The mature will discern that the Spirit may be responding to the prayer by alerting us to the trials in *living dissed.*

47

Living Dissed and the Discerning Heart

Yet lowering our arms momentarily out of weariness is not the same as lowering them for good, overcome by chronic discontent and by a listlessness that parches the soul.
—Pope Francis

Any serious follower of Jesus Christ in America today is likely to feel a "chronic discontent." Face it: we are distressed about what is reported as an erosion of religion in our culture. We are really disturbed about what seems to be the progressive dissolution of our Catholic Church—fewer people at Mass on Sunday, schools closing, parishes being combined, broken marriages, fewer priests, few or no nuns, our young disaffiliating. Our feeling dissed "momentarily out of weariness" is bad enough, but it gets worse when it warps into *living* dissed, "a chronic discontent." It does precisely that in a lot of people's experience, and it becomes a spiritual desolation, "a listlessness that parches the soul."[244]

The experiences of being dissed pile up on us in a culture that becomes more secular and less and less open to our beliefs. The society around us ignores any thought of eternal life and reduces morality to what is merely right instead of what is good. Sometimes I just turn away from the newspaper, really disheartened by so much violence. And I really feel for my family, whose young (in their thirties now) seem to live with "a general sense of disorientation," just doing what everyone is doing now and even thinking and feeling like everyone else.[245] Plenty of days, I have to struggle not to be desolate all day long.

I get down just thinking about it, but several points are worth considering. First, being dissed is a normal experience. It is not, however, a sin. So, for instance, I read an article in a national newspaper this weekend which did not report any news about clerical pederasty but simply mused one more time—one more time—on onc of the tired, vile stories. My being disgusted with the media's harping on pederasty was not, itself, a sin. But who has not followed the media's negativity and judged the American bishops pretty bluntly? This harsh judgment is a sin (*judge not*) and does not seem to have led much to praying for the bishops or to demanding to hear their experience in these inexpressibly sad events. This is an instance of how being dissed opens us to temptation.

Second, though feeling dissed is not a sin, embracing the feeling and entertaining disses leads to living dissed. This may not be a sin either—though where is *always be joyful . . . in all things, give thanks*? (1 Thess. 5:16, 18, NJB). But it makes us very liable to sin. People who have not yet found their help and hope in Christ handle the dissed life by plunging into success, wealth, and financial and physical security. They lubricate their strenuous efforts with alcohol and other drugs and a lot of luxury and pleasures. For the affluent nonbeliever, living dissed is just an aggravation.

Mature disciples are not likely to consciously embrace being desolate. If we consider some feelings of being dissed as normal, however, we readily embrace them, and they become steady states on our way. We know of a lot of instances. A woman who goes to daily Mass told me she thinks it's normal to be *disappointed* in a failing adult son. Maybe so, but it prevented her from finding a way to be compassionate with him, as our heavenly Father is compassionate. Fussing at him was getting them nowhere. Another instance: a colleague of mine in a former workplace willingly risked months of work helping Ebola victims in Africa. Yet in his situation (red state, academic) he takes it as normal to embrace *disdain* toward jihadists. As easily happens, that has turned into hatred for Muslims, a feeling that does not belong in a Christian heart.

> Mature disciples are not likely to consciously embrace being desolate. If we consider some feelings of being dissed as normal, however, we readily embrace them.

For many of us, it has become normal to go from one end of the month to another *disassociated* from the Church. This paves the way for temptation to go solo, to do it on my own, and then to unbelief. Too many of us live constantly *dissatisfied* with our lives and our gifts. That may not start out as a sin, but it easily grows into ingratitude against God's generosity, which is a big sin. Feeling dissed is not a sin; accepting it as normal in my life, though, makes me liable to fall into sin in many ways.

At the same time, the mature disciple discerns that the experience of living dissed can be either a motivating force or a temptation, can lead either to good or to evil. For the Holy Spirit can give us the experience of being dissed as an alarm about how we are thinking, feeling, or acting. That colleague who found himself hating Muslims because of jihadists had to wonder whether he believed Jesus' exhortation to *love your enemies.*

A lawyer who was disgusted with himself when he woke up with a hangover finally understood that he was being invited by a good spirit to consider his abuse of alcohol. He did. He called as I was checking these paragraphs and mentioned that he had just come from his regular AA meeting. When I am disgusted with myself for overeating, I can take that as a movement of a good spirit leading me to avoid doing it the next time the opportunity comes up.

The mature disciple can discern that being dissed is a sign of our times in which God speaks to us and the Spirit guides us. We also acknowledge that living dissed is not the Way. If we keep experiencing disses every day—and we can anticipate that we will—then perhaps that is part of our taking up our cross. We might keep in mind the parable of the weeds in the field.

Jesus said: *The one who sows the good seed is the Son of Man; the field is the world, and the good seed are the children of the kingdom* (Matt. 13:37–38). The children are surrounded by weeds, just as we are when tempted to chronic discontent and a kind of parched soul. *So you have pain now,* Jesus told his friends, *but I will see you again, and your hearts will rejoice, and no one will take your joy from you* (John 16:22).

48

Living Dissed with Authority

I ask God to give us more politicians capable of sincere and effective dialogue aimed at healing the deepest roots—and not simply the appearances—of the evils in our world!

—Pope Francis

Pope Francis has noticed the danger to our nation of having its citizens live dissed in ordinary life. For instance,

- in the common good of the nation: "While the earnings of a minority are growing exponentially, so too is the gap separating the majority from the prosperity enjoyed by those happy few."[246]
- in the home: the "individualism of our postmodern and globalized era favors a lifestyle" that "distorts family bonds."[247]
- in the Church: How can we ignore "that many people feel disillusioned and no longer identify with the Catholic tradition"?[248]
- in our daily life: faithful Catholics are "disillusioned with reality, with the Church and with themselves" and the clergy suffer a "tense, burdensome, dissatisfying" fatigue.[249]
- in our neighborhoods: instead of being "places of encounter and solidarity" they are "places of isolation and mutual distrust." We build walls to distance and protect ourselves, not connect and integrate with others.[250]

Note the words—which are the cognates in the original Spanish—*distorted, disillusioned, discontent, dissatisfied, distrust,* and *distance.*

It is tiresome to stay on the topic, but we should note that revelation tells us something very pertinent about it. Americans could add one truly inexhaustible source of dissing as the new millennium began: our public life, politics, economy, and finances. A Congress frozen in polarities. A governor's banal grandiosity sending soldiers to protect the Texas border from children. A public organization that accepts federal funds supplying abortions, for all practical purposes, on demand. Insulting half-truths on FOX and MSNBC—these seep into our hearts and leave us disaffected from civil life—and discouraged from paying just taxes. We are discouraged by the erosion of middle-class life. We are dissatisfied with the economy; what cost a dollar a short while ago now costs three or four for no reason we can see. We are dismayed by the violence in our cities and the disorder in our schools.

The mature disciple does not ignore these public realities; we all feel them. At this time in the United States' history, devout Catholics and Evangelicals—even some Catholic bishops—are torn by anxiety over health insurance, illegal immigrants, and fear of international terrorists. Now, these are grave issues, and every adult ought to have some ideas and convictions about them. But when we live dissed, we do not easily remember our first great discernment and trust our Father. We neglect turning to God to beg for help.

> For decades I had been praying mainly for victory for my candidates in elections, which often left me dissatisfied and sometimes angry.

I certainly felt my failure when I read in *The Joy of the Gospel* that Pope Francis asks God "to give us more politicians capable of sincere and effective dialogue aimed at healing the deepest roots—and not simply the appearances—of the evils in our world!"[251] For decades I had been praying mainly for victory for my candidates in elections, which often left me dissatisfied and sometimes angry. It took a while before my head got into my heart and I began to offer *supplications, prayers, intercessions, and thanksgivings . . . for kings and all who are in high positions, so that we may lead a quiet and peaceable life in all godliness and dignity* (1 Tim. 2:1–2).

I had to repent of my excessive dissatisfaction and anger, just as I had to repent of things I said and did during the Vietnam peace movement. For our Master instructed us, *Do not let your hearts be troubled* (John 14:1). During the Vietnam years, I was certainly letting my heart be troubled. Right now, even the mature can easily let our hearts be troubled. For what Ronald Reagan pointed out as the need to correct sprawling governmental programs has been transmogrified into a feeling that any government whatsoever is an intransigent problem. A report from Pew Research Center began with this sentence: "American people continue to distrust the government."[252] It's not that we are practicing eternal vigilance, the price of liberty. No. We disdain and despise government itself. The wise are correctly dismayed that our leaders have instilled into ordinary people's minds and hearts a distrust of the leaders' own authority.

By now, you'd have to look hard to find any mature disciple who has St. Paul's attitude: since all government comes from God, the civil authorities were appointed by God, so anyone who resists authority is rebelling against God's decision (see Rom. 13:1–2). We have no reason to think that St. Paul would have excepted democratic government from *civil authorities appointed by God*. We remember the kind of government Paul was dealing with, one that could be cruel and oppressive, sometimes to the Church. If he could write these instructions in his time, we do well to listen to them in ours.

Ken, let's call him, is a mature disciple, a devout Catholic with whom I used to trade e-mails about political issues. Not anymore. He has been so deeply disturbed by what he sees as disastrous developments that he cannot listen to other convictions and opinions without feeling rancor. We tend to keep off topics of public interest, which is not a satisfactory way to be friends. It may be that I push too hard (well, does the pope?). But it is mainly because Ken, who has a doctorate in business, defends the absolute autonomy of the market and sees nothing wrong with financial speculation. This seems pretty clearly to be ideology; those who hold it effectively "reject the right of states, charged with vigilance for the common good, to exercise any form of control."[253]

Too many good disciples today are constantly upset and angry over public policy issues. What was the mindset of the congressman who yelled out, "You lie!" at the president of the United States during the formal address to the Congress? What level of disquiet, discontent, and disgust could bring a serious man, in a formal situation, to blurt out a deeply offensive judgment in a loud shout, shaming himself and the Congress? That condition of soul is what we need to think of as living dissed so we can recognize that it can lead us into temptation.

The sources we—at least a lot of us—look to for our information and judgments add to the disaffection of many. FOX News has a well-defined mindset toward the government, the economy, and the safety net; it is not amicable. So has MSNBC, which is not amicable at the other end of the spectrum. But the mature disciple listens to the Church's conviction: "Politics, though often denigrated, remains a lofty vocation and one of the highest forms of charity, inasmuch as it seeks the common good."[254] With that in mind, we know what we can demand of them and what we need to beg God for.

But keeping a clear head and quiet spirit demands a lot. The earliest disciples of the risen Lord knew this challenge. So the first pope taught that their consciences ought to reflect the light of the Good News. In the first papal encyclical, 1 Peter, we find these verses of instruction:

- *For the sake of the Lord, accept the authority of every human institution: the emperor, as the supreme authority,*
- *and the governors as commissioned by him to punish criminals and praise those who do good.*
- *You are slaves of no one except God, so behave like free people, and never use your freedom as a cover for wickedness.*
- *Have respect for everyone and love for your fellow-believers; fear God and honor the emperor* (1 Pet. 2:13, 14, 16, and 17, NJB). Or the president, or the governor, or the judge. Here is a good beginning for escape from living dissed into spiritual maturity, because God—who has blessed our nation abundantly—"reveals himself in the historical mystery of our movement through grace and sin."[255]

Touchstones

- The mature disciple knows spiritual desolation and appreciates its importance.
- The core of desolation is a dimming of faith, a weakening of hope, and a coldness or absence of love. Desolation can be rooted in and manifested in head or heart or hands.
- Being dissed—disgusted, disillusioned, discouraged, and many other daily experiences—is not a sin in itself. Mature disciples can think of it as a current form of spiritual desolation.
- The experience of being dissed can lead to virtue or to sin.
- Feeling dissed is not a sin; accepting it as normal in our life, though, makes us liable to fall into sin in many ways.
- While not necessarily a sin, living dissed makes us more liable to sin: for instance, to anger, ingratitude, and resentment.
- The Holy Spirit may let us feel dissed to call our attention to an unholy belief, feeling, or action.
- The current public feeling in the United States looks a lot like living dissed. It is leading to rancor, unrest, and violence.
- We need to respect our public authorities and to pray for good men and women to enter politics.

The Capital Sin of Sloth

Most of us think that sloth is just laziness. It is that, but it is much more than that. St. John Cassian, writing on the topic more than fifteen hundred years ago, saw monks who suffered from sloth, which he called *acedia*. Their attitudes were restless, idle, careless in their living, and discontented with prayer. Does any of that sound familiar?

St. Thomas Aquinas pointed to what the slothful do: sluggish in mind, weary at work, ineffectual, they "neglect to begin the next good thing." He sees sloth as an "oppressive sorrow" in the heart that offends against the love of God. We see some slothful people try to escape this sorrow by working incessantly and irrationally. They are workaholics, driven and exhausted. "Far from a content and happy tiredness, this is a tense, burdensome, dissatisfying and, in the end, unbearable fatigue."*

At its root, sloth is the unwillingness or the inability to say yes to the gifts that God is giving me. It is despising them (I'm only five feet tall) or refusing to develop them (I hate practice) or neglecting to enact them (Smart people don't read the whole book). Slothful people can be lazy or ineffectual. They can be diffident and lack self-care. They can also be fierce workaholics—desperate to prove that "I am worth *something*."

Sloth also stains our spiritual lives. Especially today, when the Church is calling all of us to the new evangelization, "many lay people fear that they may be asked to undertake some apostolic work and they seek to avoid any responsibility that may take away from their free time." The discerning disciple realizes that this is understandable. We also know that it is not acceptable, especially among those of us who are particularly gifted with freedom, plenty, education, and a great nation to roam in.

*The citations here are from Pope Francis, *The Joy of the Gospel*, in or near para. 82.

PART ELEVEN

THE BIG AND GLORIOUS PICTURE

49

We Discerning Secularists

The immense importance of a culture marked by faith cannot be overlooked; before the onslaught of contemporary secularism an evangelized culture, for all its limits, has many more resources than the mere sum total of believers.

—Pope Francis

Reading the signs of the times accurately to discern their meaning makes demands on our heads and our hearts. One of the wisest thinkers to work at this is the Catholic philosopher Charles Taylor.[256] He notes three areas where secularism has affected us: our government, our social lives, and our religious lives.

First, our government was understood by our founders to have been founded under God. Its laws were based on our human nature and were confirmed by our nature's God. That's right out of our Declaration of Independence. We are grateful that the United States was the first nation to separate the governments of church and state. This separation certainly did not harm the Church, which created a complete school system from kindergarten to PhD and hundreds of hospitals. The separation does not seem to have harmed the state either—at least, until now. The United States is still a world power, and we have the highest statistics in the Western world for religious belonging, believing, and practice.

But secularism has leached religion out of our constitutional government. Supreme Court justices, including the late Antonin Scalia, are legal positivists and do not think that they have to keep the natural law in mind when they judicate—a very different approach from that of Jefferson and Washington.[257]

After two centuries of encouraging it, praying in public-funded schools became unconstitutional. Catholic hospitals are sued for not offering abortion, and Christian fundamentalists are required to issue same-sex marriage licenses. This is state secularism, the imposition of duties impinging on religious and conscience conviction. The changes are dense and hard to understand. But unbelievers aggressively work to get all faith and religion out of public life into private life. We now face a concerted and determined effort to make atheism the public face of the United States of America.[258]

But as is clear in everyday life, secularism has changed more than the government. It has also changed the atmosphere, secondly, of what Taylor calls "the public sphere." Those who recall the decade after the Second World War will remember how family, religion, and nation meshed into a wonderful context for "the American dream," being realized in the new suburban culture. The family reared the young as believers and as citizens. Religion "was the source of the values that animated both family and society." And the United States was "the realization and bulwark of the values central to both family and churches."[259]

This firm triangle has been quite undone. The family is under severe stress, and many young are not reared at all. The churches have been hit by scandals and are losing their hold on public affairs. And the state now sanctions things unthinkable in the very recent past: abortion, same-sex marriage, a culture of gun ownership, staggering excesses in imprisonment, and risky concentrations of wealth and fiscal power. We have found that the pope was correct: "If we remove faith in God from our cities, mutual trust would be weakened, we would remain united only by fear, and our stability would be threatened."[260] We live with a fierce insistence on individual rights. Christmas has become a frenzy of consumerism; it is barely religious anymore. We are keenly and perhaps grievously aware of how far our culture has moved into secularism.

Does this matter? Well, the secularizing spirit has touched Christ's disciples in two ways: as persons and as communities. To acknowledge it is not to be somehow disloyal to the Church or doubt its teaching. In fact, during his visit to the United States, Pope Francis said to the American bishops, "These changes affect all of us, believers and non-believers alike. Christians are not 'immune' to the changes of their times."[261] Every one of us is personally secularized in many ways. We can grow alarmed about it, particularly when the confusion keeps our young from embracing our faith firmly and steadily. But the mature disciple recognizes that letting our hearts be troubled is a temptation. The Spirit is calling us to get beyond that and do something.

For though this "public sphere" secularism affects each individual Christian first, it goes on to affect our parishes and dioceses, our schools and our associations. St. John Paul II saw clearly that "secularism . . . with its ubiquitous tentacles, succeeds at times in putting Christian communities themselves to the test."[262]

The secularizing spirit has touched Christ's disciples in two ways: as persons and as communities.

Consider this: Several generations ago, a child born into the Church was shaped in the parents' faith as certainly as he or she was drawn to speak their native English, Blackfoot, or Spanish. Families were known for their religion—even for their parish. There were always exceptions, of course. But in our grandparents' time, "mixed marriages" were quietly done in the sacristy. In 1929, that's where my parents were married, because my father was Episcopalian. Such practices kept Catholic separateness icily clear, but it marred our common life. That's over, replaced with something perhaps as bad: "The process of secularization tends to reduce the faith and the Church to the sphere of the private and personal."[263]

Yet, the discerning follower of Jesus recognizes that the stress laid on us by secularism can be relieved only in community, in communion. We all want to *belong*. A wise permanent deacon feels that the millennials, those between about nineteen and thirty-four, a lot of them our young Catholic parents, are looking for a church "where they can do good and meaningful things, where they can love others, where they can experience God in relationship and community."[264] The deacon is not sure we are serving them well.

Mature disciples feel that, as the Church, we are clearly failing ourselves in this. We need cohorts, groups, prayer circles, communities to belong to loyally, liturgies that weave joyful personal connections—and we are not finding or creating those at all adequately. Yet, we know the truth: "The important thing is to not walk alone, but to rely on each other as brothers and sisters, and especially under the leadership of the bishops, in a wise and realistic pastoral discernment."[265] As we discern how to move in this, we have to recognize that we are swimming against the mighty current of our individualistic, rights-ridden, secular culture.

This culture has eroded our good intentions, and we have to struggle against the feeling that our religion is our personal affair, period. We need to listen to Pope Francis when he insists: "The immense importance of a culture marked by faith cannot be overlooked," even as we face "the onslaught of contemporary secularism," because our culture has been marked by faith from its beginning and "has many more resources than the mere sum total of believers."[266] We individualists, however, need a change of heart about our private religious life if we are to change our lives as Catholics in the public sphere. Cardinal Donald Wuerl argued that "the transformation of society begins with conversion" of individuals, which "essentially involves discernment."[267] The change goes on to create communities of people with converted minds and hearts—quite plainly the work the Spirit is calling us to do.

A lot has to change in our heads and our hearts before we learn how to hold hands and be grateful.

50

How Do I Know I Am Grateful?

Thanks to faith we have come to understand the unique dignity of each person, something which was not clearly seen in antiquity.
—Pope Francis

He had everything, and he was grateful. During a retreat, Theodore told me that he wondered sometimes whether his "being grateful" was just "being glad" that his business was a success and made him rich. Even the way he said this revealed that this issue was a temptation for him. We worked through head, heart, and hands—to the radiant truth: if I am rich, and I neither embezzled funds nor robbed widows but simply did the next good thing, this wealth, at least for now, is God's gift to me.

Still—maybe his gratitude was fortified by his happiness at being rich, the way coffee is fortified by chicory? A lot of Americans need discernment here, because some commentators mistakenly claim that Jesus condemned the rich—and we are all pretty rich in one way or another. All of us have to be as discerning as Theodore. So we must consider what discernment has to do with gratitude.

Begin with the hands—with what the grateful among God's people do. The people of the old covenant offered to God gifts taken from the choice things of the flock and field. These they placed on the altar and burned up. They did this to show God the Lord that the people had discerned that God had given them enough—more than enough. They could sacrifice the best of it in praise and thanksgiving. The American people as a whole keep up something like that: last year, the nation gave to good works a sum as great as the GDP of the nation of Denmark.[268]

As God grew more and more intimate with his people, he pushed their thanksgiving out of the sanctuary and away from possessions and into daily life and relationships. *He has told you, O mortal, what is good,* prophesied the prophet Micah. *And what does the LORD require of you but to do justice, and to love kindness, and to walk humbly with your God?* (Mic. 6:8).

The mature disciple understands what *sacrifice* means now. As St. Augustine put it, a sacrifice is any human action that puts us in filial, loving communication with God our Lord. Hence, standing in God's presence, calling to mind that divine love is giving me life, and thanking God for these gifts—that is a sacrifice of praise. This is the first work of our hands, and if we keep it in our hearts, it is what has been termed—in endearing yet clunky wording—the "attitude of gratitude."

The grateful person, consequently, rarely envies others' goods and gifts. Envy and jealousy are spiritual fevers rising out of the unholy infection of feeling that my life is paltry or that I am inadequate to the life given me (basically, the capital vice of sloth). I remember admiring how a very adequate businessman felt visibly delighted to hear that another man in the same line of business had had to expand his operation. The businessman felt no jealousy for the other because he plainly did not feel inadequate and was content that he had enough.

Gratitude does not leave much room in our hearts for abiding anger either. During a penance service a while back, a middle-aged sales manager confessed to me that he was confused about why he lashed out in anger all the time. He was pretty hefty, and I fleetingly pictured his colleagues cowering. But he was vexed at himself: what was the anger *about*? After some exploring, he saw plainly: he was not content with what he had achieved—very adequate though it was—and he did not really like himself. His problem might have been clinical, caused by illness or mental/emotional problems, but neither of us thought so. He had sunk into the capital sin of pride, feeling that he was a little god. When others didn't recognize his god-ness, he shot out his Zeus-like flashes of lightning. I prayed that his colleagues would see the clouds pass as he got a better sense of himself.

Gratitude must rest on a true sense of self, a sense that what I am and what I have are enough. If I am grateful to God, I can live this day with joy, because gratitude is happiness multiplied by wonder, a phrase we remember from G.K. Chesterton. We are delighted to find that what we are and have is wonderful and surprising. Like the little lad who asked his beloved granny how old she was. Eighty. "*Eighty?*" he cried. "Did you start-ed at *one?*"

Gratitude must rest on a true sense of self, a sense that what I am and what I have are enough.

Gratitude *walks humbly with your God.* The humble do not take things for granted. To take for granted does not mean "to take as a gift"; it means "to be expected as my right." The grateful person does not take good fortune or wealth or success or happiness for granted but receives them as gifts.

Our faith asks us to "come to understand the unique dignity of each person."[269] The mature disciple knows to begin this understanding with the self. Without a holy self-appreciation, we can hardly "love our neighbor *as ourselves.*" And in my experience, a lot of anger with "our neighbor" is rooted in this lack of grateful self-appreciation.

As it matures, gratitude leads to acknowledgment and the enactment of the gifts (charisms) I have, even if they reach out to others in organization, governance, and leadership. I once directed an elderly, elegant religious woman who recounted to me her various careers. She was sent early to learn counseling, when the Church was absorbing the new signs of the times flashing from Vatican II. She found herself—literally, found herself—having to conduct several of the congregation's schools through the explosion of technology—as well as epochal shifts in the lives of the teenaged girls in her charge. She was sent oversees to teach and to form younger religious and then to run programs of renewal for religious and priests.

In all of these capacities, she did solid, enduring work. And all along, she lived in a mild desolation because she felt little interior appreciation for her gifts of organization and leadership. She had been wounded early on because the leadership of her congregation placed a lot of emphasis on scholastic abilities. She was not a scholar; she was an organizer and a leader of real talent.

Considering carefully over long months of prayer what God had accomplished in and through her, she came to feel content at her life. More than that, she grew clear about the strength she displayed in facing really tough challenges. When we first started meeting, she laughed a lot, but it was a nervous laugh. She didn't smile much at all. Now she smiles a lot. She still laughs, too, and keeps on being grateful.

51

Discernment at the Wake

Instead of seeming to impose new obligations, [Christians] should appear as people who wish to share their joy, who point to a horizon of beauty and who invite others to a delicious banquet.

—Pope Francis

All humankind gazes at the horizon named death. The people of the covenant did. *The souls of the just are in the hands of God*, wrote the author of the book of Wisdom (3:1). Christians often read these words at our own requiem Masses. But the author of Wisdom did not know, or even suspect, what we have been given to discern about death and dying. Here are two thoughts the discerning disciple ought to keep handy so we can be joyful at the wake.

First, our faith is clear: the souls of the just are always in the hands of the Lord—not just when we die, but always. At every moment, in all situations, God's Spirit cherishes us. Does the earth's atmosphere caress our lungs and nourish our blood with oxygen? Does gravity gently hold us down to the earth? Just so does God's Spirit caress us, gently drawing us into life and showing us what to appreciate, desire, and do. We do not need a lot of laws. St. Augustine admonished his fellow bishops not to make too many canons and rubrics; they are nothing but a burden to the holy People of God. For we are given the gifts of wisdom, understanding, piety, and awe of the Lord—and we grow mature as we enact those gifts in freedom.

There is a second revelation that the author of the book of Wisdom could not even dream of. He imagined that the just souls in God's hands were pale remnants of the living person. But we know that our dead are not shadows of their real selves. They are live selves.

Those who refuse to believe in the resurrection see no further than Scripture's obvious remark that *here we have no lasting city* (Heb. 13:14). We live in the first "temporary housing" of all. Temporary, but very promising, as Pope Francis pointed out. As he said, the resurrection was not merely a historical event. The resurrection is an ongoing act of God's almighty, all-wise power. We believe in our hearts what the writer of Job could not even dream of: we believe in the resurrection of the dead. We are flesh destined to endure beyond the endtime. We are already living in the risen humanity established by Jesus when he died and rose again, banishing death.

He has banished death for each one of us. As Jesus explained it, *the will of him who sent me, that I should lose nothing of all that he has given me*—that's us—*but raise it up on the last day*—not only the last day of all days but the personal last day at which each of us will arrive (John 6:39).

On the day we die, our souls will separate from our physical selves and leave time. This separation of spirit and body is no new thing—only its suddenness will be new. Carefully consider this: over our lifetime, our whole self thrives as a maturing soul in a steadily changing body. Not theory, this is fact: we grow a whole new body every seven years, new blood and bones, new atoms and molecules, different from before—and yet we remain ourselves.

Our bodies are slowly renewed every seven years. But then, at death, our soul separates suddenly from our physical self and takes up a different way of relating with the mud of earth. This new way is nothing sorrowful or diminished. In truth, it is a glorious way far beyond the "horizon of beauty" we look to. It is the way Jesus rose from the dead in his own body: the way he can be with his friends wherever they are, even locked up in a room; the way he can prepare a breakfast to share with them on the seashore; the way Mary can cling to him; and the way he can press Thomas's hand to his chest at the wound.

Today, it is the way he can open the Scriptures to our minds and make us a people "who point to a horizon of beauty and who invite others to a delicious banquet."[270] Maybe all those dinners with the rich gave Jesus what he needed to fantasize about this heavenly banquet. I have no trouble imagining it—I just have Eggs Sardou at New Orleans's Panola Street Café.

Meanwhile, sipping our coffee and chicory, we wait for the day appointed for us. If our death is already in us as cancer or heart disease or failing liver, we may feel like the disciples when Jesus suddenly showed up again: afraid. When the body is separating from the soul in dying, it produces physical effects that can rise to our consciousness as fear. I saw that happen in the huge failing body of a dying priest. He was a gracious and complex man, a moral theologian. The whole Jesuit community loved "Big Ed." As I anointed him the day before he died, I could see in his eyes that he was handling fear. He had no reason to indulge that fear or embrace it, because for him, Jesus was not a force or a historical development. For him, as for all of us, Jesus is *You.*

We'd better not wait until we are dying to turn to that *You.* We need to grow mature in our relationship with him, to address him and listen to him. Every one of us must. The disciple young in maturity may doubt that we can grow in this grace of knowing Jesus intimately; the foolish may doubt that the relationship is real at all. But the disciple who has matured in his or her discerning can stay busy opening the self more and more to encounter him, personally, daily, without fear. So Pope Francis wrote the first sentence in his exhortation: "The joy of the Gospel fills the hearts and lives of all who encounter Jesus. Those who accept his offer of salvation are set free from sin, sorrow, inner emptiness and loneliness."

We can be most secure of our love for that *You* who is Jesus Christ when we feel deeply and enact carefully the friendships and loves that God places in our lives. If feeding the hungry is really feeding Jesus himself, how much more is loving his people really loving Jesus himself? This love-in-action grounds true Christian happiness. "We achieve fulfilment when we break down walls and our heart is filled with faces and names!"[271]

Our communion in Christ is not intangible, merely a felt emotion and nothing more. Our communion has hands and eyes, limbs and hearts.

Our communion in Christ is not intangible, merely a felt emotion and nothing more. Our communion has hands and eyes, limbs and hearts. Our communion is with the saints—the saints who are all around us. This is the truth, and those who believe it easily do what St. Paul told the Thessalonians to do: *Always be joyful; pray constantly; and for all things give thanks; this is the will of God for you in Christ Jesus* (1 Thess. 5:16–18, NJB).

So we pray and thank God and are joyful even at the wake, because we can see over a far horizon of beauty. *The kingdom of heaven may be compared to a king who gave a wedding banquet for his son* (Matt. 22:2). It is, indeed, "a wonderful thing to be God's faithful people."[272]

Touchstones

- The founders of our nation were acting "under God" and believed that our laws were rooted in divine law.
- State secularism imposes irreligion by forcing actions contrary to citizens' consciences. It destroyed Russia and other nations.
- Secularism in America affects each disciple and the Church by transforming religion into a private matter.
- We must reverse the effects of secularism in religion by forming strong cohorts and communities.
- The mature disciple has developed an "attitude of gratitude."
- We fear death neither as part of life nor as punishment for sin. We face death as one more way of joining Jesus Christ.
- We live joyful because beyond this horizon an eternal banquet of love is prepared for us.

The Examen of the Future

The Examen is part of our tradition. Usually thought of in terms of St. Ignatius's *Spiritual Exercises*, it has emphasized watching sins and failings. That emphasis was deepened by our post-Enlightenment emphasis on rules and counting things.

The whole thrust of discernment as a spirituality for the twenty-first century has parted from that. We have opened ourselves deliberately and boldly to finding how the Holy Spirit is leading us here and now. Before we get lost in a haze, we might note that the Spirit has given us very concrete, defined norms to guide our head, heart, and hands: the Spirit's gifts.

Mature discernment brings us to recognize and enact the gifts of the Holy Spirit. Saying yes to them is one thing; doing them is another. For these gifts are virtues, powers, or authorities. They are like spiritual muscles: exercise them, practice them, and they grow stronger. Do not, and they grow weak.

Here is the proper matter for the Examen in the twenty-first century: all the gifts of the Holy Spirit. Take the first gifts of faith, hope, and love. Spend a day or a week—or a longer time if you are weak in it—practicing that virtue. Then patiently work through wisdom, understanding, counsel, fortitude (courage), piety, knowledge, and fear of the Lord. Or do what one couple did after I explained this to them: they made a flipchart with "the virtue of the day," which causes a bit of merriment.

But never think that living these virtues is merely of personal interest. "These gifts are meant to renew and build up the Church."* Pope Francis's gifts are surely building up the Church. And wouldn't the Church in my place and time be wonderfully attractive if all of us went through the week displaying the "fruit of the Spirit," walking in love, joy, peace, patience, kindness, goodness, trustfulness, gentleness, and self-control?

The Examen of the future is the Gifts Examen.

*Pope Francis, *The Joy of the Gospel*, para. 130. The Scripture is Galatians 5:24.

Endnotes

1. Antonio Spadaro, SJ, "Big Heart Open to God," *America*, September 30, 2013, http://americamagazine.org/pope-interview.
2. Pope Francis, *The Joy of the Gospel* (Frederick, Md.: The Word Among Us, 2013), 149. Also available in *Evangelii Gaudium* at w2.vatican.va/content/vatican/en.html.
3. Steve Scherer, "Pope Francis Says Hypocrisy Undermines Church's Credibility," *Reuters*, April 14, 2013, uk.reuters.com/article/2013/04/14/.
4. Pope Francis, *The Church of Mercy* (Chicago: Loyola Press, 2014), 56.
5. The author is not identified. "Why This Waste?" *The Word among Us* (July 2015): 5.
6. Francesca Ambrogetti and Sergio Rubin, *Pope Francis: Conversations with Jorge Bergoglio* (New York: G. P. Putnam's Sons, 2013), 57. This seems to be the only interview he gave until he began responding to reporters on his travels as pope.
7. Antonio Spadaro, SJ, "Big Heart Open to God," *America*, September 30, 2013, http://americamagazine.org/pope-interview.
8. http://americamagazine.org/pope-interview.
9. Pope Francis, *Open Mind, Faithful Heart: Reflections on Following Jesus* (New York: Crossroad Publishing Company [Herder & Herder], 2013) 126.
10. See Jules J. Toner, SJ, *A Commentary on Saint Ignatius' Rules for the Discernment of Spirits* (St. Louis: Institute of Jesuit Sources, 1982) and *What Is Your Will, O God?* (St. Louis: Institute of Jesuit Sources, 2004). Edward Malatesta, SJ, ed., *Discernment of Spirits* (Collegeville, Minn: The Liturgical Press, 1970). Timothy M. Gallagher, O.M.V., *The Discernment of Spirits*, (New York: The Crossroad Publishing Company, 2005). William A. Barry SJ, *A Friendship Like No Other: Experiencing God's Amazing Embrace* (Chicago: Loyola Press, 2008).
11. *Gaudium et Spes, The Church in the Modern World* (1965), para. 4, w2.vatican.va/content/vatican/en.html. The expression shows up only this once in the thick volume of conciliar documents.
12. Cardinal Donald Wuerl, "Pass It On," *America* (February 28, 2011): 12.

13. *Catechism of the Catholic Church*, paragraph 1780.

14. Luke Timothy Johnson, "A Modus Vivendi?" *Commonweal* (January 13, 2012): 17. Also available at http://digitalcommons.fairfield.edu/.

15. Richard Gaillardetz, "Magisterium and the Faithful," *America* (September 24, 2012): 16.

16. Dr. Eileen Rafaniello Barbella, lecture handout, 2012.

17. Lawrence D. Gillick, SJ, cited in Joseph A. Tetlow, SJ, "Ignatian Spirituality Conference," *National Jesuit News*, April/May 2005, 21.

18. Dr. Edmund D. Pellegrino, "Evangelium Vitae, Euthanasia, and Physician-Assisted Suicide," *Choosing Life: A Dialogue on Evangelium Vitae*, ed. Kevin Wm. Wildes, SJ, and Alan C. Mitchell (Washington, D.C.: Georgetown University Press, 1997), 243.

19. Antonio Spadaro, SJ, "A Big Heart Open to God," *America*, September 30, 2013, http://americamagazine.org/pope-interview.

20. *Gaudium et Spes, The Church in the Modern World* (1965), para. 4, w2.vatican.va/content/vatican/en.html.

21. Pope Francis, Homily at Casa Santa Marta, April 16, 2013, http://en.radiovaticana.va/. Accessed February 2, 2015.

22. Pope Paul VI, Apostolic Exhortation *Evangelii Nuntiandi*, para. 43, w2.vatican.va/content/vatican/en.html.

23. Saint John Paul II, Apostolic Exhortation *Pastores Dabo Vobis*, paragraph 10, w2.vatican.va/content/vatican/en.html. Cited in Pope Francis, *The Joy of the Gospel* (Frederick, Md.: The Word Among Us, 2013), 116.

24. Pope Francis, *The Church of Mercy: A Vision for the Church* (Chicago: Loyola Press, 2014).

25. Pope Francis, *The Joy of the Gospel* (Frederick, Md.: The Word Among Us, 2013), 75. Also available in *Evangelii Gaudium* at w2.vatican.va/content/vatican/en.html.

26. Ibid., 71. Also available in *Evangelii Gaudium* at w2.vatican.va/content/vatican/en.html, para. 89.

27. Second Vatican Council, *Lumen Gentium*, (November 21, 1964), part 2, para. 9, w2.vatican.va/content/vatican/en.html.

28. Antonio Spadaro, SJ, "Big Heart Open to God," *America*, September 30, 2013, http://americamagazine.org/pope-interview.

29. Ibid.

30. Pope Francis, *Open Mind, Faithful Heart* (New York: Crossroad Publishing Company, 2013), 126.

31. Antonio Spadaro, SJ, "Big Heart Open to God," *America*, September 30, 2013, http://americamagazine.org/pope-interview.

32. Ibid.
33. Pope Francis, *Open Mind, Faithful Heart* (New York: Crossroad Publishing Company, 2013), 46.
34. Pope Francis, quoted in Anthony Faiola, "Pope Lectures Catholic Elders at Closing of Synod on Family," *Washington Post*, October 25, 2015, www.washingtonpost.com/world/europe/.
35. Pope Francis, *The Joy of the Gospel* (Frederick, Md.: The Word Among Us, 2013), 180. Also available in *Evangelii Gaudium* at w2.vatican.va/content/vatican/en.html.
36. http://w2.vatican.va/content/francesco/en/apost_exhortations/documents/
37. Pope Francis, Address to Brazilian Leaders (Rio de Janeiro, July 27, 2013), w2.vatican.va/content/vatican/en.html.
38. International Theological Commission, "Sensus Fidei in the Life of the Church," (2014), paras. 2 and 3, w2.vatican.va/content/vatican/en.html.
39. Pope Francis, *The Joy of the Gospel* (Frederick, Md.: The Word Among Us, 2013), 23. Also available in *Evangelii Gaudium* at w2.vatican.va/content/vatican/en.html.
40. Ibid., 189.
41. Second Vatican Council, *Lumen Gentium* (November 21, 1964), para. 12, w2.vatican.va/content/vatican/en.html.
42. *Catechism of the Catholic Church*, para. 1780.
43. Pope Francis, *The Joy of the Gospel* (Frederick, Md.: The Word Among Us, 2013), 13. Also available in *Evangelii Gaudium* at w2.vatican.va/content/vatican/en.html.
44. Ibid., 189.
45. Pope Francis, "The Courage of the Cross," *Open Mind, Faithful Heart* (New York: Crossroad Publishing Company, 2013), 72.
46. Pope Francis, *The Joy of the Gospel* (Frederick, Md.: The Word Among Us, 2013), 54. Also available in *Evangelii Gaudium* at w2.vatican.va/content/vatican/en.html.
47. Ibid., 180.
48. Ibid., 189.
49. Ibid., 34.
50. Antonio Spadaro, SJ, "Big Heart Open to God," *America*, September 30, 2013, http://americamagazine.org/pope-interview.
51. Glenn R. Schiraldi, PhD, *The Self-Esteem Workbook* (Oakland, Calif: New Harbinger Publications, 2001); Jay E. Adams, *The Biblical View of Self-Esteem, Self-Love, and Self-Image* (Eugene, Ore: Harvest House Publishers, 1986). See also David D. Burns, MD, *Ten Days to Self-Esteem* (New York: Quill/HarperCollins, 1993, 1999). Burns's sensible writing helped define this movement.

52. Pope Francis, quoting Pope Benedict XVI, in *Laudato Si'*, para. 65. https://w2.vatican.va/content/en/encyclicals/documents/papa-francesco_20150524_enciclica-laudato-si.html.

53. Pope Francis, *The Joy of the Gospel* (Frederick, Md.: The Word Among Us, 2013), 40. Also available in *Evangelii Gaudium* at w2.vatican.va/content/vatican/en.html.

54. Walter Ciszek, SJ, with Daniel Flaherty, SJ, *He Leadeth Me* (New York: Doubleday, 1973; reissued by Ignatius Press, 1995), 79.

55. Antonio Spadaro, SJ, "Big Heart Open to God," *America*, September 30, 2013, http://americamagazine.org/pope-interview.

56. Ibid.

57. Pope Francis, *The Joy of the Gospel* (Frederick, Md.: The Word Among Us, 2013), 59. Also available in *Evangelii Gaudium* at w2.vatican.va/content/vatican/en.html.

58. Ibid, 88.

59. Ibid., 60.

60. Ibid., 10.

61. Antonio Spadaro, SJ, "Big Heart Open to God," *America*, September 30, 2013, http://americamagazine.org/pope-interview.

62. Pope Francis, *The Joy of the Gospel* (Frederick, Md.: The Word Among Us, 2013), 131. Also available in *Evangelii Gaudium* at w2.vatican.va/content/vatican/en.html.

63. Ibid., 10.

64. Walter Ciszek, SJ, with Daniel Flaherty, SJ, *He Leadeth Me* (New York: Doubleday, 1973; re-issued by Ignatius Press, 1995), 79–80.

65. Pope Francis, *The Joy of the Gospel* (Frederick, Md.: The Word Among Us, 2013), 131. Also available in *Evangelii Gaudium* at w2.vatican.va/content/vatican/en.html.

66. Ibid., 132.

67. Ibid., 132.

68. Ibid., 132–33.

69. Ibid., 133.

70. Ibid., 134.

71. Ibid., 135, 131.

72. Ibid., 136.

73. Ibid., 184.

74. Ibid., 182.

75. Ibid., 17.

76. Ibid., 186.

77. Ibid.

78. Pope Francis, Address to the Fifth Convention of the Church in Italy (November 10, 2015), https://w2.vatican.va/content/francesco/en/speeches/2015/november/documents/papa-francesco_20151110_firenze-convegno-chiesa-italiana.html.

79. Pope Francis, *The Joy of the Gospel* (Frederick, Md.: The Word Among Us, 2013), 186. Also available in *Evangelii Gaudium* at w2.vatican.va/content/vatican/en.html.

80. Ibid., 34.

81. Pope Francis, *The Church of Mercy* (Chicago: Loyola Press, 2014), 121.

82. Pope Benedict XVI, *Deus Caritas Est* (2005), para. 1; cited in Pope Francis, *The Joy of the Gospel* (Frederick, MD: The Word Among Us, 2013), 14. Also available in *Evangelii Gaudium* at w2.vatican.va/content/vatican/en.html.

83. Pope Francis, *The Joy of the Gospel* (Frederick, Md.: The Word Among Us, 2013), 9. Also available in *Evangelii Gaudium* at w2.vatican.va/content/vatican/en.html.

84. Ibid., 71, 72.

85. Ibid., 72.

86. Carlo Maria Martini, *Journeying with the Lord* (Alba House, 1987), 462.

87. Pope Francis, *The Joy of the Gospel* (Frederick, Md.: The Word Among Us, 2013), 188. Also available in *Evangelii Gaudium* at w2.vatican.va/content/vatican/en.html.

88. Ibid., 190.

89. Ibid., 70.

90. Ibid., 70.

91. Ibid., 146, 71.

92. Ibid., 71.

93. Pope Paul VI, *Evangelii Nuntiandi,* Apostolic Exhortation, 1975, para. 61.

94. Pope Francis, "United by the Grace of Memory," *Open Mind, Faithful Heart* (New York: Crossroad Publishing Company, 2013), 103.

95. Ignatius Loyola, *Spiritual Exercises* [193], italics added. All citations are taken from Louis J. Puhl, SJ, *The Spiritual Exercises of St. Ignatius*, Loyola University Press, Chicago, 1951.

96. Ignatius Loyola *Spiritual Exercises,* [203], italics added.

97. Pope Francis, *The Joy of the Gospel* (Frederick, Md.: The Word Among Us, 2013), 26. Also available in *Evangelii Gaudium* at w2.vatican.va/content/vatican/en.html.

98. Ibid., 87.

99. St. John Paul II, *Familiaris Consortio,* "On the Role of the Christian Family in the Modern World" (November 22, 1981), para. 5, w2.vatican.va/content/vatican/en.html.

100. Pope Francis, *The Joy of the Gospel* (Frederick, Md.: The Word Among Us, 2013), 91. Also available in *Evangelii Gaudium* at w2.vatican.va/content/vatican/en.html.
101. Pope Francis, Address to the Fifth Convention of the Church in Italy, https://w2.vatican.va/content/francesco/en/speeches/2015/november/documents/papa-francesco_20151110_firenze-convegno-chiesa-italiana.html.
102. Antonio Spadaro, SJ, "A Big Heart Open to God," *America*, September 30, 2013, http://americamagazine.org/pope-interview.
103. Pope Francis, *The Joy of the Gospel* (Frederick, Md.: The Word Among Us, 2013), 57. Also available in *Evangelii Gaudium* at w2.vatican.va/content/vatican/en.html.
104. Ibid., 57.
105. St. John Paul II, *Familiaris Consortio*, "On the Role of the Christian Family in the Modern World" (November 22, 1981), para. 5, w2.vatican.va/content/vatican/en.html. The pontiff said this particularly of Christian spouses and parents.
106. Jens Manuel Krogstad, "114th Congress Is Most Diverse Ever," *FactTank: News in Numbers*, January 12, 2015, Pew Research Center, http://www.pewresearch.org.
107. Pope Francis, *The Joy of the Gospel* (Frederick, Md.: The Word Among Us, 2013), 188. Also available in *Evangelii Gaudium* at w2.vatican.va/content/vatican/en.html.
108. Antonio Spadaro, SJ, "A Big Heart Open to God," *America*, September 30, 2013, http://americamagazine.org/pope-interview.
109. Pope Francis, *Open Mind, Faithful Heart* (New York: Crossroad Publishing Company, 2013), 101.
110. Romans 12:2, NJB. The New International Version has "his good, pleasing, and perfect will."
111. See www.pray-as-you-go.org or www.pray.com.au or the earliest of these sites, www.sacredspace.ie.
112. Pope Francis, *The Joy of the Gospel* (Frederick, Md.: The Word Among Us, 2013), 128. Also available in *Evangelii Gaudium* at w2.vatican.va/content/vatican/en.html. The pope's point here is that the whole course of evangelization, from prayer to preaching to penitence, rises out of the Word of God.
113. Matthew 5:48, NJB. The NRSVACE reports the more standard translation: *Be perfect, therefore, as your heavenly Father is perfect.*
114. Pope Francis, *The Joy of the Gospel* (Frederick, Md.: The Word Among Us, 2013), 180. Also available in *Evangelii Gaudium* at w2.vatican.va/content/vatican/en.html. The pope is drawing on St. John Paul II's Apostolic Letter *Novo Millennio Ineunte*, 6 January 2001, paragraphs 32–34.
115. Antonio Spadaro, SJ, "A Big Heart Open to God," *America*, September 30, 2013, http://americamagazine.org/pope-interview.
116. Ibid.

117. Pope Francis, *Laudato Si', Encyclical on Care for Our Common Home* (May 24, 2015), para. 73, http://w2.vatican.va/content/francesco/en/encyclicals/documents/papa-francesco_20150524_enciclica-laudato-si.html.

118. Pope Francis, "The Embrace of God's Mercy: Homily for the Mass for the Possession of the Chair of the Bishop of Rome," Pope Francis, *The Church of Mercy: A Vision for the Church* (Chicago: Loyola Press, 2014), 3.

119. Pope Francis, "Address on Fear of the Lord," Wednesday General Audience (June 11, 2014), w2.vatican.va/content/vatican/en.html.

120. Pope Francis, *Laudato Si', Encyclical on Care for Our Common Home* (May 24, 2015), para. 73, http://w2.vatican.va/content/francesco/en/encyclicals/documents/papa-francesco_20150524_enciclica-laudato-si.html.

121. Pope Francis, *The Church of Mercy: A Vision for the Church* (Chicago: Loyola Press, 2014), vii.

122. Pope Francis, "Address on Fear of the Lord," Wednesday General Audience (June 11, 2014), https://zenit.org/articles/english-summary-of-pope-s-audience-on-fear-of-the-lord/.

123. Pope Francis, Weekly Audience, 11 June 2014, https://zenit.org/articles/english-summary-of-pope-s-audience-on-fear-of-the-lord/.

124. Pope Francis, "Homily Opening the Extraordinary Synod of Bishops on the Family, October 5, 2015." http://en.radiovaticana.va.

125. *Catechism of the Catholic Church*, para. 1.

126. Pope Francis, *The Joy of the Gospel* (Frederick, Md.: The Word Among Us, 2013), 185. Also available in *Evangelii Gaudium* at w2.vatican.va/content/vatican/en.html.

127. Ibid., 188.

128. Ibid., 91.

129. Ibid., 20.

130. Ibid., 20.

131. Ibid., 147.

132. 1 Cor. 7:7. This whole chapter shows St. Paul shifting among what he thinks, what he feels, and what he and others in various states in life do. He is not reporting what Christ taught him but applying it to Christian sexual maturity in everyday life.

133. Pope Francis, "Called Despite Our Fears," *Open Mind, Faithful Heart* (New York: Crossroad Publishing Company, 2013), 35.

134. *Catechism of the Catholic Church*, para. 2392.

135. Pope Francis, *Open Mind, Faithful Heart* (New York: Crossroad Publishing Company, 2013), 68.

136. Pope Francis, "Address to Bishops," Rio de Janeiro, Brazil (July 27, 2013), www.zenit.org/en/articles/francis-address-to-bishops.

137. See Ernest Becker, *The Denial of Death* (New York: Simon & Schuster, 1973). Becker's book is still much consulted. He argues that our civilization is what the psychiatrists call "a defense mechanism" against the death-terror, and only heroism allows us to remain sane in the face of it.

138. Harley Quinn, "Denial of Death and Depression," *The Thinking Atheist* (August 27, 2011), www.thethinkingatheist.com/forum/Thread-Denial-of-Death-and-depression.

139. Pope Francis, *The Joy of the Gospel* (Frederick, Md.: The Word Among Us, 2013), 183. Also available in *Evangelii Gaudium* at w2.vatican.va/content/vatican/en.html.

140. Steve Jobs, "Stanford Commencement Speech" (June 12, 2005), www.businessinsider.com.

141. Mona Simpson, "A Sister's Eulogy for Steve Jobs," *New York Times*, October 30, 2011, http://www.nytimes.com/2011/10/30/opinion/mona-simpsons-eulogy-for-steve-jobs.html.

142. *Catechism of the Catholic Church*, paragraph 399. The next tragic consequence: "They become afraid of the God of whom they have conceived a distorted image."

143. See James C. Hefley and Marti Hefley, *By Their Blood: Christian Martyrs from the Twentieth Century and Beyond* (Grand Rapids: Baker Books, 2004).

144. See the comprehensive study of this by Robert Royal, *The Catholic Martyrs of the Twentieth Century: A Comprehensive World History*, New York, Crossroad, 2006.

145. Pope Francis, *The Joy of the Gospel* (Frederick, Md.: The Word Among Us, 2013), 183. Also available in *Evangelii Gaudium* at w2.vatican.va/content/vatican/en.html.

146. This happened at the still-functioning Academy of the Sacred Heart, Grand Coteau, Louisiana. Her sickroom is preserved there, the only shrine in the United States at the location of a certified miracle.

147. *Catechism of the Catholic Church,* paragraph 989.

148. Ibid., paragraph 992. "God revealed the resurrection of the dead to his people *progressively*" (italics added).

149. Ibid., paragraph 996.

150. See John 11:25; *Catechism of the Catholic Church*, para. 1002.

151. Pope Francis, *The Joy of the Gospel* (Frederick, Md.: The Word Among Us, 2013), 190. Also available in *Evangelii Gaudium* at w2.vatican.va/content/vatican/en.html.

152. Ibid., 190.

153. Galatians 1:16, NJB. The *New American Bible* translates this as "to me," which is the other standard translation. This "in me" reveals more of St. Paul's experience of Christ and helps us understand how we live and move and have our being in him: he comes to us, not vice versa. And "*Christ in me*" makes clear that when Jesus sends us as the Father sent him, he sends us not to *have a mission* but to *be a mission.*

154. Francesca Ambrogetti and Sergio Rubin, *Pope Francis: Conversations with Jorge Bergoglio* (New York: Penguin Random House, 2013), 29.

155. Francesca Ambrogetti and Sergio Rubin, *Pope Francis: Conversations with Jorge Bergoglio* (New York: Penguin Random House, 2013), 172.

156. Pope Francis, Morning Homily at Casa Santa Marta, October 15, 2013, https://zenit.org/articles/pope-francis-love-of-god-and-neighbor-heals-you-of-idolatry-and-hypocrisy/.

157. Pope Francis, *The Joy of the Gospel* (Frederick, Md.: The Word Among Us, 2013), 48. Also available in *Evangelii Gaudium* at w2.vatican.va/content/vatican/en.html.

158. Pope Francis, Morning Homily at Casa Santa Marta, October 15, 2013, http://en.radiovaticana.va.

159. Pope Francis, *The Joy of the Gospel* (Frederick, Md.: The Word Among Us, 2013), 51. Also available in *Evangelii Gaudium* at w2.vatican.va/content/vatican/en.html.

160. Ibid., 48.

161. See the very informative, if rather difficult, criticism of this change by Roberto Mangabeira Unger in his *Passion: An Essay on Personality* (New York: The Free Press, 1984).

162. See Timothy M. Gallagher, O.M.V., *The Examen Prayer: Ignatian Wisdom for Our Lives Today* (New York: Crossroad Publishing Company, 2006); and Jim Manney, *A Simple, Life-Changing Prayer: Discovering the Power of St. Ignatius Loyola's Examen* (Chicago: Loyola Press, 2011).

163. See Joseph Tetlow, SJ, *The Most Postmodern Prayer: American Jesuit Identity and the Examen of Conscience, 1920–1990* (St. Louis: Institute of Jesuit Sources, 1994).

164. George Aschenbrenner, SJ, "The Consciousness Examen," *Review for Religious* 31, no. 1 (1972), 14–21. Full text at Loyola Press website: www.ignatianspirituality.com.

165. John Paul II, *Pastores Dabo Vobis*, para. 10. This is "Gospel discernment" that interprets the meaning of a situation. "Interpretation is a work which is done in the light and strength provided by the true and living Gospel, which is Jesus Christ, and in virtue of the gift of the Holy Spirit."

166. Pope Francis, "Walking" (Address to the Clergy in the Cathedral of San Rufino in Assisi, October 4, 2013) in *The Church of Mercy* (Chicago: Loyola Press, 2014), 75.

167. Mark Thibodeaux, SJ, *Reimagining the Ignatian Examen* (Chicago: Loyola Press, 2015).

168. Ibid., xvii.

169. Pope Francis, *Laudato Si', Encyclical on Care for Our Common Home* (May 24, 2015), para. 116, http://w2.vatican.va/content/francesco/en/encyclicals/documents/papa-francesco_20150524_enciclica-laudato-si.html.

170. Pope Francis, "Walking," *The Church of Mercy* (Chicago: Loyola Press, 2014), 75.

171. Pope Francis, *The Joy of the Gospel* (Frederick, Md.: The Word Among Us, 2013), 188. Also available in *Evangelii Gaudium* at w2.vatican.va/content/vatican/en.html.

172. Ibid., 187.

173. Pope Benedict XVI, *Deus Caritas Est* (2005), para. 16, w2.vatican.va/content/vatican/en.html.

174. Pope Francis, *The Joy of the Gospel* (Frederick, Md.: The Word Among Us, 2013), 188. Also available in *Evangelii Gaudium* at w2.vatican.va/content/vatican/en.html. To Francis, *encounter* is a very important word in part because "faith is an encounter with Jesus" (Pope Francis, *The Church of Mercy* [Chicago: Loyola Press, 2014], 99).

175. Francesca Ambrogetti and Sergio Rubin, *Pope Francis: Conversations with Jorge Bergoglio* (New York: Penguin Random House, 2013), 57.

176. Pope Francis, *Laudato Si', Encyclical on Care for Our Common Home* (May 24, 2015), para. 107, http://w2.vatican.va/content/francesco/en/encyclicals/documents/papa-francesco_20150524_enciclica-laudato-si.html.

177. See Richard Dawkins, *The Blind Watchmaker* (New York: W. W. Norton, 1986) and *The God Delusion* (New York: Houghton Mifflin, 2006).

178. Francesca Ambrogetti and Sergio Rubin, *Pope Francis: Conversations with Jorge Bergoglio* (New York: Penguin Random House, 2013), 57.

179. Antonio Spadaro, SJ, "A Big Heart Open to God," *America*, September 30, 2013, http://americamagazine.org/pope-interview.

180. Pope Francis, *Laudato Si', Encyclical on Care for Our Common Home* (May 24, 2015), para. 113, http://w2.vatican.va/content/francesco/en/encyclicals/documents/papa-francesco_20150524_enciclica-laudato-si.html.

181. Pope Francis, *Laudato Si'*, para. 203.

182. Antonio Spadaro, SJ, "A Big Heart Open to God," *America*, September 30, 2013, http://americamagazine.org/pope-interview.

183. *Catechism of the Catholic Church*, para. 387: "Only the light of divine Revelation clarifies the reality of sin and particularly of the sin committed at mankind's origins."

184. Pope Francis, Speech at the Presidential Palace, Manila, January 16, 2015, americamagazine.org/content/dispatches.

185. Pope Francis, *The Joy of the Gospel* (Frederick, Md.: The Word Among Us, 2013), 51. Also available in *Evangelii Gaudium* at w2.vatican.va/content/vatican/en.html. Note that Francis did not condemn "unbridled capitalism" but "unbridled consumption."

186. Ibid., paragraph 60.

187. Ibid., 196.

188. Pope Francis, "Address to the Bishops of Brazil," Rio de Janeiro, July 28, 2013, w2.vatican.va/content/vatican/en.html.

189. Pope Francis, *The Joy of the Gospel* (Frederick, Md.: The Word Among Us, 2013), 41–42. Also available in *Evangelii Gaudium* at w2.vatican.va/content/vatican/en.html.

190. See Charles Duhigg, *The Power of Habit: Why We Do What We Do in Life and Business* (New York: Random House, 2012). See also Bernard Haring, *The Truth Will Set You Free*, vol. 2, *Free and Faithful in Christ* (New York: Crossroad Publishing Company, 1979).

191. Tracy Wilkinson, "Pope Francis Visits Rehab Hospital, Decries Drug Legalization," *Los Angeles Times*, July 24, 2013, http://articles.latimes.com/2013/jul/24/world/la-fg-wn-pope-francis-drugs-20130724.

192. Antonio Spadaro, SJ, "A Big Heart Open to God," *America*, September 30, 2013, http://americamagazine.org/pope-interview.

193. *Gaudium et Spes, The Church in the Modern World* (1965), para. 16, w2.vatican.va/content/vatican/en.html. The expression shows up only this once in the thick volume of conciliar documents.

194. *Catechism of the Catholic Church*, paras. 1783 and 1784.

195. Pope Francis, "Address to the Bishops of Brazil," July 28, 2013, w2.vatican.va/content/vatican/en.html.

196. Pope Francis, "The Hardening of Hearts," *Open Mind, Faithful Heart* (New York: Crossroad Publishing Company, 2013), 120.

197. Pope Francis, "Address to the Bishops of Brazil," July 28, 2013, w2.vatican.va/content/vatican/en.html.

198. Pope Francis, *The Joy of the Gospel* (Frederick, Md.: The Word Among Us, 2013), 45. Also available in *Evangelii Gaudium* at w2.vatican.va/content/vatican/en.html.

199. Ibid., 45.

200. Ignatius Loyola, *Spiritual Exercises*, [313–336].

201. Pope Francis, *The Joy of the Gospel* (Frederick, Md.: The Word Among Us, 2013), 191. Also available in *Evangelii Gaudium* at w2.vatican.va/content/vatican/en.html.

202. Ibid., 45.

203. Ibid., 68.

204. Ibid., 191.

205. See Aaron T. Beck, MD, *Cognitive Therapy and the Emotional Disorders* (Madison, Conn: International Universities Press, 1975). Dr. Aaron Beck is the founder of cognitive therapy. During the 1960s and 1970s, Beck's cognitive therapy model moved us to see that thoughts, feelings, and behavior are closely linked. Early on, most of us began reflecting on the "thoughts" and focused on "self-image," "concepts of God," and "ideas of holiness."

206. See Martin E. P. Seligman, *Authentic Happiness: Using the New Positive Psychology to Realize Your Potential for Lasting Fulfillment* (New York: Free Press, 2002).

207. Pope Francis, *The Joy of the Gospel* (Frederick, Md.: The Word Among Us, 2013), 192. Also available in *Evangelii Gaudium* at w2.vatican.va/content/vatican/en.html.

208. Ibid., 192.

209. Pope Francis, *Laudato Si', Encyclical on Care for Our Common Home* (May 24, 2015), para. 220, http://w2.vatican.va/content/francesco/en/encyclicals/documents/papa-francesco_20150524_enciclica-laudato-si.html.

210. *Catechism of the Catholic Church*, para. 1644; Matthew 19:6.

211. Antonio Spadaro, SJ, "A Big Heart Open to God," *America*, September 30, 2013, http://americamagazine.org/pope-interview.

212. Ibid.

213. Pope Francis, *The Joy of the Gospel* (Frederick, Md.: The Word Among Us, 2013), 193. Also available at Also available in *Evangelii Gaudium* at w2.vatican.va/content/vatican/en.html.

214. Gelpi thought of the Spirit as *She* and wrote to explain it. See Donald L. Gelpi, SJ, *The Divine Mother: A Trinitarian Theology of the Holy Spirit* (University Press of America, 1984). I found it convincing and think that we could well look into discerning the Spirit as manifesting the feminine in God.

215. Antonio Spadaro, SJ, "A Big Heart Open to God," *America*, September 30, 2013, http://americamagazine.org/pope-interview.

216. Ephesians 2:10. NJB replaces "we are what he has made us" with the better known and more vivid "We are God's work of art."

217. Pope Francis, *The Joy of the Gospel* (Frederick, Md.: The Word Among Us, 2013), 67. Also available in *Evangelii Gaudium* at w2.vatican.va/content/vatican/en.html.

218. David Van Biema, "Mother Teresa's Crisis of Faith" *Time*, August 23, 2007, http://time.com

219. Pope Francis, "Pope to Hungarian Consecrated: Spread God's Consolation," September 18, 2015, at https://zenit.org/en/articles/pope-to-hungarian-consecrated-spread-god-s-consolation.

220. Pope Francis, *The Joy of the Gospel* (Frederick, Md.: The Word Among Us, 2013), 143. Also available in *Evangelii Gaudium* at w2.vatican.va/content/vatican/en.html.

221. Kevin Burke, SJ, *Pedro Arrupe: Essential Writings* (Maryknoll, New York: Orbis Books 2004), 57.

222. Pope Francis, *The Joy of the Gospel* (Frederick, Md.: The Word Among Us, 2013), 13. Also available in *Evangelii Gaudium* at w2.vatican.va/content/vatican/en.html.

223. St. Ignatius Loyola, *Spiritual Exercises,* "Rules for Discernment of Spirits II," [335]. The words in quotation marks are a free translation.

224. Pope Francis, "Pope to Hungarian Consecrated: Spread God's Consolation," September 18, 2015, at https://zenit.org/en/articles/pope-to-hungarian-consecrated-spread-god-s-consolation.

225. Brother Lawrence, *The Practice of the Presence of God,* compiled and edited by Rev. Joseph de Beaufort. The book is still being printed, now ecumenically.

226. Ignatius Loyola, *Spiritual Exercises,* [175].

227. Whitney Belprez, "Agnostic Convert," www.whyimcatholic.com. This website was founded by lay Catholics in 2011.

228. Pope Francis, "Humility and Hope," in *Open Mind, Faithful Heart* (New York: Crossroad Publishing Company, 2013), 94.

229. Ibid.

230. According to the National Centers for Disease Control. Suicide is a stark reality in our culture. It is the tenth leading cause of death among adults and the third most common death of those between ages 15 and 24.

231. Ignatius Loyola, *Spiritual Exercises,* [317].

232. *The Catechism of the Catholic Church* offers excellent summary statements of our faith in "Marriage in the Lord," 1612–17; and "The Celebration of Marriage," 1621–24.

233. Pope Francis, *The Joy of the Gospel* (Frederick, Md.: The Word Among Us, 2013), 47. Also available in *Evangelii Gaudium* at w2.vatican.va/content/vatican/en.html.

234. Ibid., 47. In this place, Pope Francis considers a sin our "crude and naïve trust in the goodness of those wielding economic power and in the sacralized workings of the prevailing economic system. Meanwhile, the excluded are still waiting."

235. Ignatius Loyola, *Spiritual Exercises,* [317].

236. Typical sports headline: "Epic Response! J. K. Rowling Claps Back at Fan Who Disses Serena Williams Following Wimbledon Win." Even Harry Potter knows the word now.

237. Pope Francis, *The Joy of the Gospel* (Frederick, Md.: The Word Among Us, 2013), 59. Also available in *Evangelii Gaudium* at w2.vatican.va/content/vatican/en.html.

238. Pope Francis, "United by the Grace of Memory" in *Open Mind, Faithful Heart* (New York: Crossroad Publishing Company, 2013), 103.

239. Pope Francis, *The Joy of the Gospel* (Frederick, Md.: The Word Among Us, 2013), 191. Also available in *Evangelii Gaudium* at w2.vatican.va/content/vatican/en.html.

240. Ibid., 44.

241. Ibid., 52.

242. Ibid., 45.

243. Pope Francis, *Open Mind, Faithful Heart* (New York: Crossroad Publishing Company, 2013), 103.

244. Pope Francis, *The Joy of the Gospel* (Frederick, Md.: The Word Among Us, 2013), 191. Also available in *Evangelii Gaudium* at w2.vatican.va/content/vatican/en.html.

245. Ibid., 54.

246. Ibid., 48.

247. Ibid., 56.

248. Ibid., 59.

249. Ibid., 67, 66.

250. Ibid., 62. About the cities, the pope begins, "We cannot ignore the fact that in cities human trafficking, the narcotics trade, the abuse and exploitation of minors, the abandonment of the elderly and infirm, and various forms of corruption and criminal activity take place."

251. Ibid., 149.

252. Pew Research Center, "How Americans View Government," March 10, 1998, www.people-press.org.

253. Pope Francis, *The Joy of the Gospel* (Frederick, Md.: The Word Among Us, 2013), 48. Also available in *Evangelii Gaudium* at w2.vatican.va/content/vatican/en.html. The pope adds this sobering judgment: "A new tyranny is thus born, invisible and often virtual, which unilaterally and relentlessly imposes its own laws and rules."

254. Ibid., 149.

255. Pope Francis, "God's Plan Unveiled," in *Open Mind, Faithful Heart* (New York: Crossroad Publishing Company, 2013), 126.

256. See Charles Taylor, *A Secular Age* (Cambridge, Mass.: Harvard University Press, 2007).

257. Anthony Giambrone, O.P., "Who Is to Judge? The legal philosophies of Antonin Scalia and Thomas Aquinas," *America*, March 21, 2016. Also at http://americamagazine.org/issue/who-judge.

258. See Taylor, Part IV: Narratives of Secularization. Taylor's work was finished a decade ago—the decade during which most of the changes listed here were completed. Commenting on Richard Dawkins's and other materialists sense of wonder at nature, Taylor remarks that "the piety verges perhaps on the 'religious,'" 606.

259. Charles Taylor, *A Secular Age* (Cambridge, Mass.: Harvard University Press, 2007), 506.

260. Pope Francis, *Lumen Fidei*, para. 54, w2.vatican.va/content/vatican/en.html.

261. Pope Francis, "Address to Bishops Attending the World Meeting of Families," September 27, 2015, w2.vatican.va/content/vatican/en.html.

262. St. John Paul II, *Evangelium Vitae*, March 25, 1995, para. 21, w2.vatican.va/content/vatican/en.html.

263. Pope Francis, *The Joy of the Gospel* (Frederick, Md.: The Word Among Us, 2013), 54, Also available in *Evangelii Gaudium* at w2.vatican.va/content/vatican/en.html.

264. Deacon Jay Cormier, "A Deacon's Education," *America* (September 28, 2015): 16.

265. Pope Francis, *The Joy of the Gospel* (Frederick, Md.: The Word Among Us, 2013), 33. Also available in *Evangelii Gaudium* at w2.vatican.va/content/vatican/en.html. We can observe that American bishops are not yet very active in this particular pastoral discernment, but we have to do it humbly, since none of us is, either.

266. Pope Francis, *The Joy of the Gospel*, paragraph 68.

267. Cardinal Donald Wuerl, "Pass It On," *America* (February 28, 2011): 12.

268. The 79.7 million Catholics, in the last year, through parishes, charitable organizations like St. Vincent de Paul, soup kitchens, and all the rest, gave about $30 billion to charity. This drawn from the Pulitzer Prize-winning website Politifact (www.politifact.com).

269. Pope Francis, *Lumen Fidei*, w2.vatican.va/content/vatican/en.html.

270. Pope Francis, *The Joy of the Gospel* (Frederick, Md.: The Word Among Us, 2013), 20. Also available in *Evangelii Gaudium* at w2.vatican.va/content/vatican/en.html.

271. Ibid., 189.

272. Ibid.

About the Author

Joseph A. Tetlow, SJ, has practiced, taught, and written on discernment since before Vatican II. He is a spiritual director and has led numerous retreats for laypeople on the topic of discernment. Often hailed as a world authority on Ignatian spirituality, Fr. Tetlow is the author of many books, including *Making Choices in Christ* and *Choosing Christ in the World.*